Beginner's Guide To The Sun

Peter O. Taylor • Nancy L. Hendrickson

Front cover: The Stonehenge Monument near Wiltshire, England, frames the rising Sun at the summer solstice (photograph courtesy of L. C. Smith).

Rear cover: The arch of the McMath Solar Telescope profiles the Sun in the early morning twilight at National Solar Observatory facilities on Kitt Peak, Arizona (photograph courtesy of National Optical Astronomy Observatories).

Cover design by Kristi Ludwig.   Book design by Mark Watson.

Printed in the United States of America

Publisher's Cataloging-in-Publication Data
(Prepared by Quality Books Inc.)

Taylor, Peter O.
      Beginner's guide to the sun / Peter O. Taylor,
Nancy L. Hendrickson.
      p. cm.
      Includes bibliographical references and index.
      ISBN 0-913135-23-2

      1. Sun—Popular works. I. Hendrickson,
Nancy L. II. Title.
QB521.4.T39 1995   523.7
                            QBI95-20093

Contents

Preface

There's real excitement in today's research of the Sun, made possible through the fascinating studies undertaken by the dedicated amateur and professional astronomers of the past. It doesn't take long to realize that as recently as the American Civil War very little was known about solar dynamics. In the following century discoveries progressed by leaps and bounds; yet the recent flight of the Ulysses spacecraft above the Sun's polar regions clearly demonstrates that many questions remain to be answered.

There's excitement too in learning that solar observations by serious amateur astronomers can still be useful to the professional solar community. Not many other areas of scientific endeavor are so open to the conscientious nonprofessional. This is one arena where you can make a meaningful scientific contribution by careful daily observations, using only a modest telescope equipped with a minimum of accessories. In fact the famous Wolf telescope, responsible for many thousands of sunspot observations at the Swiss Federal Observatory in Zurich, Switzerland, has only 80 millimeters of aperture. If, after reading this book, you're caught up in the excitement of solar observation, we've provided the information needed to get you started with ease and safety.

Because of the time lag between finished manuscript and publication, it's nearly impossible to be entirely up to date, especially when describing the science of Space Age solar astronomy. However, we have tried to include the most timely information available to us. If we have succeeded, it's due in large part to the generous assistance of the professional solar scientists and others listed below. Considering the subject, we think it's entirely appropriate that a portion of our information came to us through the electronic superhighway from sites available to all on the Internet (Project 3). The authors have in fact carried on a several-year electronic correspondence—never meeting face to face—writing the book entirely via electronic mail.

Many people have aided us in this project. They include Richard Thompson of IPS Radio and Space Services in Sidney, Australia; Helen Coffey of National Geophysical Data Center; David Rust of Applied Physics Laboratory, Johns Hopkins University; Sara Martin of Big Bear Solar Observatory and Helios

Research; Karen Harvey, Frank Recely, and Jeremy Wagner of Kitt Peak National Solar Observatory; Matt Penn of National Solar Observatory at Sacramento Peak; John Leibacher with the GONG project; Dick Fisher and Jim Elliot of NASA's Goddard Space Flight Center and David Hathaway of Marshall Space Flight Center; Russell Howard of the Naval Research Laboratory; H. U. Keller of Rudolf Wolf Gesellschaft; Ross McCluney of the Florida Solar Energy Center; Fred Sawyer and Robert Terwilliger of the North American Sundial Society, and Ron Livesey of the British Astronomical Association. The Software Bisque allowed us to reproduce the star charts included in Project 4 with their astronomical software, The Sky; Willy Bonker computer-generated several of the project illustrations, and William Winkler provided a fine description of his hydrogen-alpha equipment and observational technique.

A large measure of appreciation is also due the individuals who helped us locate and obtain the many photographs we have included. Especially helpful were the NASA Public Information Office in Washington, D.C.; Joan Burkepile of the National Center for Atmospheric Research; Donald F. Neidig of Sacramento Peak Observatory; Ray Bowers of the Carnegie Institution of Washington; Jim Harwood of the Smithsonian Institution; Rosa Wilson of the National Park Service; and CompuServe friend Ken Spencer. A special thanks to Peter Hingley, Head Librarian, Royal Astronomical Society, for tracking down a few particularly elusive photographs and for sharing the Society's delightful tales of the extraordinary Francis Baily. Last, but certainly not least, we are grateful to L. C. Smith of Amesbury, England, whose beautiful photograph of Stonehenge graces the cover of this book.

MaryJane Taylor, Loras College and University of Wisconsin, read the manuscript and provided excellent comments and useful scientific insights. Pamela Taylor also read the manuscript, pointing out our grammatical inconsistencies and other abuses of the English language.

Finally, few such projects could be undertaken without the encouragement of family and friends. For that invaluable support and motivation, a very special thank you to Pamela, Helene Kennan, Charlene Crilley, Sharon Kahn, Eva Langer, and Vicki Fite.

—the authors—

1
Early Beliefs

In the cool pre-dawn darkness more than a thousand years ago, the Zuni Sun-priest hurried along the trail to his vantage point high on the mesa. He sang and prayed as he did each morning, awaiting his first glimpse of the Sun. Finally, as the leading rays of light burst above a distant mountain peak, the priest plotted the position of the rising Sun against the desert landscape and carefully carved a mark into a crude soft-pine calendar. Today he would announce to his people that the Sun was nearing its winter home. The winter solstice—the moment in Earth's annual journey about the Sun that marks the beginning of winter—was nearly at hand.

Of all astronomical bodies, it was the Sun that dominated the hearts and lives of our early ancestors. But since a true understanding of this familiar but puzzling object was far beyond their grasp, they often elevated the Sun to a mythical or even divine status. And as we will learn in this and subsequent chapters, such feelings were not restricted to primitive peoples alone.

Zuni Sun-priest, Pueblo of Zuni, New Mexico, circa 1896. Even today, astronomer-priests stand on mesa tops at dawn, carefully marking the location of the rising Sun. *Photograph courtesy of the Smithsonian Institution, Photo Number 2250.*

The legendary Sun

Nestled between the Tigris and Euphrates Rivers, ancient Babylonians thought of the Sun as a living being, the giver of law, who emerged each morning through a door in the east only to disappear in the west as night fell. Their neighbors to the west, the Egyptians, bestowed divinity

This Egyptian carving on stone, dating from the fifth century B.C., shows Nut, the goddess of the sky, arched over the Earth. At right and left of the disk are two boats. Egyptian astronomers believed that the Sun made a hidden journey by boat each night, traveling from the western to the eastern horizon. *Photograph courtesy of the Metropolitan Museum of Art. Gift of Edward S. Harkness, 1914 (14.7.1).*

on the Sun, asserting that Re, their Sun god, sailed across the sky by celestial ship each day and then descended into the dark underworld at night. There Re engaged in terrifying encounters with snakes and fire, but always emerged victorious each dawn.

The Bible and early Israelite texts contain surprisingly few references to the Sun other than its creation by God in the first case, and warnings against its worship in the second. However, we do know that the ancient Hindus saw it as one of a group of three high-ranking gods, named Surya, in their Books of Divine Knowledge. On the other hand, the early Eskimos believed that at night the Sun was rowed around the sky just beyond the northern horizon. In an attempt at scientific reasoning, the Eskimos cited the aurora borealis as evidence that the Sun was traveling in that vicinity.

Some, however, knew that the Sun could occasionally be frightening and unpredictable. At such times—total solar eclipses—darkness fell suddenly and unexpectedly during the daytime. Since eclipses were poorly understood by a majority of the world's people until relatively recently, they have understandably been regarded with misgiving and suspicion. The surprise generated by their occurrence has resulted in war and the end of war, political intrigue, confusion, and despair among those who unknowingly lived within the path.

The first reasonably reliable account of an eclipse is believed to be one set down by the ancient Chinese more than 4000 years ago during the Hsia dynasty. This eclipse is particularly noteworthy since it may have led to the demise of the royal Chinese astronomers, Hsi and Ho. According to a legend that has circulated through the ages, Hsi and Ho had drunk a bit too much wine as the eclipse began and failed to perform the necessary rituals to drive off the "dragon" that seemed to be devouring the Sun. Terror spread among the people, and when the emperor

This petroglyph—symbolizing the Sun—was etched into a rock cliff by the Sinagua, a prehistoric tribe who inhabited Arizona's Verde Valley. Such petroglyphs are difficult to date, but the Sinagua (or their ancestors) are known to have inhabited the Southwest United States from earlier than 1000 B.C. through A.D. 1400. *Photograph by N. L. Hendrickson.*

learned of the astronomers' antics he had the two miscreants relieved of their heads. As you might expect, no astronomer since has repeated this mistake!

Even though the early Chinese were probably the first to record a solar eclipse, the Greeks were almost certainly the first to understand why they occur. Like other ancient communities, the Greeks personalized the Sun. Early in their history they viewed the Sun in much the same way as the Egyptians did, but from about the fifth century B.C., the Sun became firmly associated with their god Phoebus Apollo. Still, at about this same time a few Greek philosophers began to question the true nature of the Sun. Many of their ideas—a small Sun, close to the Earth, or a flat Sun, supported by air—seem very strange to us today.

9

Fajada Butte. Hundreds of years ago, three sandstone slabs were placed high on a rock panel and carefully decorated with a pair of spiral petroglyphs. At the summer solstice the Sun shines between the slabs, throwing a bright sliver of light onto the center of the larger spiral. *Photograph courtesy of the National Park Service.*

Nevertheless, some of their conclusions were amazingly accurate: the curvature of the Earth, knowledge that solar eclipses occurred when the Moon moved in front of the Sun, and even Herakleides' idea that the Earth was spherical and rotated on its axis originated within the scholarly pre-Christian Greek community. The evidence is somewhat conflicting, but it may well be that the Greek scientist Thales of Miletus was the first to actually forecast an eclipse. Thales may have used the long Babylonian eclipse record to predict the solar eclipse that occurred in 585 B.C.—if accurate, a truly astounding feat for this early era.

Moreover, as early as 434 B.C., Anaxagoras had determined that the Sun was a "fiery stone" about the size of the Peloponnesus, and Pythagorean scholars provided the first theory of a planetary system orbiting a central fire. By the third century B.C., Aristarchus had concluded that this central body was in fact the Sun, and had made crude estimates of its size and distance from the Earth.

Around 130 B.C., perhaps the foremost of all ancient astronomers, Hipparchus, derived the best early estimate of the solar distance, one which would survive for many centuries. His method relied upon calculations involving measurements taken at lunar eclipse. This technique was perfectly valid in theory, and Hipparchus' estimate of the Moon's diameter was close to ours. Unfortunately, his other results varied considerably from the true values, mainly because Hipparchus vastly underestimated the difference in distance from Moon to Earth and Earth to Sun.

Politics as well as contemplation played a role in the thinking of many Near Eastern philosophers; and since the Greeks dominated all around them, their thinking held sway in neighboring nations. In fact, some achievements once attributed to early Babylonian astronomers occurred after the Greeks had invaded the valley of the Euphrates River and after the fall of Babylon in 539 B.C.—an important event which almost certainly affected future Babylonian thinking.

The ruins of Pueblo Bonita. This D-shaped structure encloses a central plaza, designed so that its rooms were shaded during the summer, while the winter Sun was reflected into the central plaza. *Photograph courtesy of the National Park Service.*

The "perfect" Sun

On the other hand, the influence of the powerful Greek philosopher Aristotle stifled intelligent thought about the cosmos. His insistence on the Sun's absolute perfection in the fourth century B.C. profoundly controlled the thought and direction of western society for over 1500 years. Moreover, the later, highly complex Ptolemaic explanation of certain planetary movements (called epicycles) within an Earth-centered, or geocentric, universe made Aristotelian thought just that much more complex.

Today we know that the long delay in European perception of the Sun's true character can be traced to the widely accepted teachings of Aristotle and his determination that the Sun was a flawless (that is, unmarked) ball of "pure fire." This declaration seems all the more startling in view of the observation of a large mark on the Sun—almost certainly a huge sunspot—by Theophrastus, who was a pupil of Aristotle himself.

The solar calendar

Long before the Zuni astronomer-priest tracked the Sun and seasons, other Native Americans had faithfully followed its movement through the daytime sky. (Even today, astronomer-priests among the Western Pueblos—Hopis in northeastern Arizona and Zunis in northwestern New Mexico—and the culturally affiliated

11

El Caracol, the ancient Maya observatory at Chichen Itza, Mexico. *Photograph courtesy of the Smithsonian Institution, Photo Number 204.*

Eastern Pueblos of the Rio Grande Valley treat skywatching as a solemn religious duty. They stand on mesa tops at dawn as their ancestors surely did, carefully marking the location of the rising Sun to determine the change of seasons.) While we don't know the exact motivation for their observations, we do know the Sun was important enough to these early tribes that they spent an extraordinary amount of time recreating its presence in petroglyphs—artistic symbols created by tediously chipping layers of "desert varnish" from the rocks along canyon walls. Such rock art, composed of spirals, concentric circles, or rayed Suns, is fairly commonplace throughout the American Southwest.

For these cultures the days marking the solstices (points in the Earth's orbit where the Sun reaches the points farthest north and south in the sky, marking the beginning of summer and winter) and equinoxes (moments during the year when day and night are of equal length) were important indicators of the passage of time and therefore spawned elaborate rituals. For instance, members of the Indian Sun Clan once gathered on the mesas of the Southwest on the day of the summer solstice—the beginning of summer, on or about June 21—to pray for plentiful rain and bountiful crops. And they believed that ritual relay races held on the same plateaus at the winter solstice would give the Sun strength to continue its long journey through time.

The Anasazi Indians, known as the "Ancient Ones," flourished in the Four Corners area (where Arizona, New Mexico, Colorado, and Utah meet) between 900 and 1300, before vanishing virtually overnight. The Anasazi developed a complex understanding of the Sun's cycles and movements and used the information to plan their farming and worship and to chronicle important events. They built elaborate structures in the name of the Sun, which they recognized as a vital part of their lives.

The remnants of many such settings can still be seen today, and they are monumental tributes to the faith of those who designed and built them. At one location

The Stonehenge site near Wiltshire, England, at the summer solstice. *Photograph courtesy of L. C. Smith, retired custodian of the Stonehenge Monument.*

named Yellow Jacket, near Cortez, Colorado, 2-meter tall rock monoliths weighing between 220 and 320 kilograms have been shaped into wedges that point to the rising Sun on the day of the summer solstice. And at Casa Rinconada—the great kiva, or special room devoted to religious ceremony, in Chaco Canyon—sunlight enters a strategically placed window and strikes a small niche in the northwest wall, an event that also marks the onset of the summer season. When we examine the history of the world's primitive civilizations, we see the solstice repeatedly marked this way.

Chaco Canyon also contains a site known as Fajada Butte. Hundreds of years ago three sandstone slabs were placed high on a rock panel and carefully decorated with a pair of spiral petroglyphs. At the summer solstice the Sun shines between the slabs, throwing a bright sliver of light onto the center of the larger spiral. While most solstice sites were mark the event at sunrise, Fajada Butte does so at midday. In addition to the depiction of the solstice, at noon on the days immediately before and afterward a separate spot of light shines directly on the smaller spiral.

The Sun's impact on ancient American cultures is represented in other ways as well, although less frequently. Another Anasazi site in northwest New Mexico contains the ruins of Pueblo Bonita, the largest of the Chacoan ruins. This D-shaped, monolithic structure encloses a central plaza split by a low wall along a line running from north to south. Pueblo Bonita has frequently been described as a "solar efficient city" because it was designed so its rooms were shaded during

13

An aerial view of the Big Horn Medicine Wheel, located at an altitude of 3000 meters in the Big Horn mountains, Wyoming. The Wheel consists of a stone circle with 28 spokes radiating from a central cairn of stones. *Photograph courtesy U.S. Forest Service.*

the summer while the heat and light from the winter Sun was reflected into the central plaza.

In addition to the monuments that track the Sun, researchers have found evidence of early stargazers' observations of other types of astronomical events in a few locations. One of the most intriguing is illustrated by an intricate rock art scene, which researchers believe represents the brilliant supernova of A.D. 1054. For several days the light from this exploding star, located many millions of millions of kilometers away, would have shone extraordinarily brightly—easily visible even in the daytime sky.

Like their northern brethren, the ancient Americans of the Southern Hemisphere displayed a vigorous interest in the Sun. In this land where the seasons are the reverse of those in the north, the Peruvian Inca of Machu Picchu once held Festivals of Renewal, or Inti Raymi, which began at the solstice. The Inca religion was itself centered on astronomically inspired worship. Inca emperors assumed they were descended from the Sun and were therefore regarded as divine. Extravagant Inca rituals were scheduled to occur during the summer solstice when, according to ancient records, their king made offerings to his father the Sun while prophecies were read from the entrails of a llama.

The study of the Sun and stars grew more sophisticated at the hands of the Maya Indians, who once prospered in what we call Mexico and Central America. The Maya erected a grand astronomical observatory called the Caracol at Chichen Itza, at one time a center of the Maya civilization. The windows at the top of the observatory's tower open toward the equinox sunset point and the most northerly and southerly settings of Venus. Observations of the Sun and other stars played important roles in the planning of this fabulous city, located high on the Yucatan Peninsula between the cities of Cancun and Merida.

Nearby, the great pyramid known as "El Castillo" was ingeniously designed so that at the vernal (spring) equinox a stream of sunlight formed a serpent that appeared to slither down the balustrade on the pyramid's northern face, eventually striking the stone serpent heads below. To the Maya, this snake of light was Kukulkan, the feathered serpent whose appearance at the equinox was seen as a blessing on the city.

Not all primitive observatories were as complex as the one at Chichen Itza, however. Half a world away, and more than 2000 years earlier, ancient Britons constructed a circular "menhir" (a prehistoric monument consisting of a single tall stone standing alone or with others) with stones precisely aligned at sunrise on the day of the summer solstice. A single tall stone, the Heel Stone, marks this important event. This monument is Stonehenge, located near Wiltshire, England. Stonehenge was built in stages between 2800 and 1100 B.C., a period extending from the late Stone Age into the Bronze Age. Unfortunately, although much has been written about unraveling the mysteries of Stonehenge, its builders left no records and little is known for certain.

The Bighorn Medicine Wheel in Wyoming is reminiscent of Stonehenge—a great stone circle with a questionable history. The Wheel is 27 meters in diameter, designed with a central cairn of stones from which radiate 28 individual spokes. Features of the Wheel align with the Sun at the solstice and with the brightest stars of midsummer dawn; thus the Wheel may have served as a primitive calendar. At the time of its discovery in 1880 by gold prospectors, the nearby Crow Indians believed the Wheel was very old indeed, placed there "before the first light came." Sadly, like Stonehenge, its true origin may well be lost in time.

Which site is likely to be the most ancient of all such structures? The answer may surprise you. Recent research indicates that the Newgrange Tomb built north of Dublin, Ireland, around 5150 years ago is the oldest monument linked to observations of the Sun's movements. The tomb is contained within a mound of loose stones about 90 meters wide and 10 meters tall. Studies show that thousands of years ago the first sunlight of the winter solstice flowed down a long central corridor and illuminated a carving made up of three spirals, a pattern that would be repeated for thousands of years by uncounted cultures in many parts of the world. Sunlight first penetrated the tomb's entrance through a small horizontal opening some 20 centimeters high and a meter wide, creating a lighted spot on the chamber floor and illuminating the carving of three spirals. At daybreak on

The Newgrange Tomb, located near Dublin, Ireland, is the oldest known structure with an astronomical function. The tomb is thought to have been built nearly 5150 years ago, thus predating Stonehenge and the Great Pyramids. Note the similarity between these spiral etchings and those featured in petroglyphs, produced thousands of years later by Native Americans in the American Southwest. *Photograph courtesy of the Irish Tourist Bureau.*

the solstice, the Sun appeared in the lower left-hand corner of the gap, then silently rose until it was centered, and eventually exited at the upper right-hand corner. The opening was carefully crafted so that when the Sun was framed within its borders it matched the Sun's width vertically within about one-tenth of the solar diameter, very good for builders 5000 years ago.

If we can learn anything from these examples, it is that for untold centuries human beings have continuously sought ways to understand the nature of the Sun and predict its behavior. It's easy to imagine why such a detailed knowledge of the solstices and other prominent features of the Sun's annual path in the sky were so important to our ancestors. Since many of the ancients had no written language, we can only guess what it would be like to live in a world with no clocks, no calendars, no simple way to decide which events might soon determine their very existence. The answers to these questions were vital to their survival but far beyond their level of understanding. As a consequence, those who could predict such things—often related to simple seasonal changes—gained enormous power and influence over their peers.

Thanks to the emergence of archaeoastronomy (the study of ancient astronomical practices), scientists are beginning to solve the secrets of these early stargazers. Whether we examine the site of the Fort Ancient Indians in Ohio, the Moose Mountain Medicine Wheel in Canada, or the Newgrange Tomb, one factor stands out above all others—the Sun, more than any other celestial body, has long intrigued humanity and been a subject of intense observation.

Intricate rituals, sacrifices meant to appease its immense importance, worship, fear, and contemplation of the Sun all were part of ancient life. The Spanish gave it the name "El Sol," the Babylonians "Shamash," and the Greeks "Helios." It was revered by virtually all primitive cultures, and for nearly two millennia most western Europeans believed it to be flawless. But regardless of the name or expectation, we have come to realize that by undertaking the first studies of the Sun our ancestors also became the first true solar astronomers.

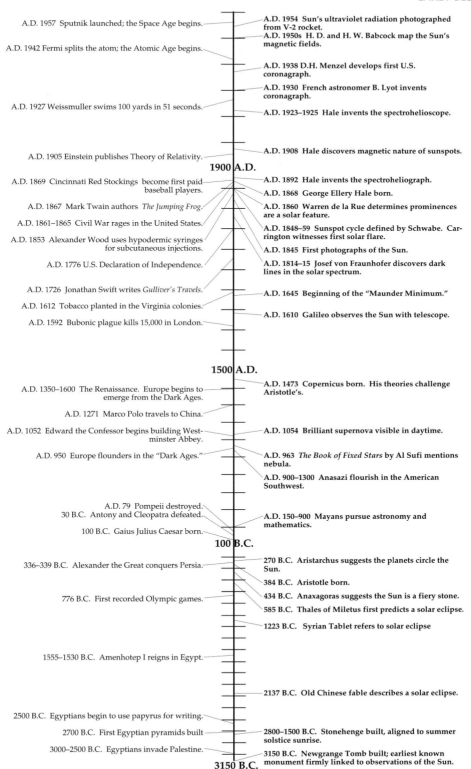

A.D. 1957 Sputnik launched; the Space Age begins.

A.D. 1954 Sun's ultraviolet radiation photographed from V-2 rocket.

A.D. 1950s H. D. and H. W. Babcock map the Sun's magnetic fields.

A.D. 1942 Fermi splits the atom; the Atomic Age begins.

A.D. 1938 D.H. Menzel develops first U.S. coronagraph.

A.D. 1930 French astronomer B. Lyot invents coronagraph.

A.D. 1927 Weissmuller swims 100 yards in 51 seconds.

A.D. 1923–1925 Hale invents the spectrohelioscope.

A.D. 1905 Einstein publishes Theory of Relativity.

A.D. 1908 Hale discovers magnetic nature of sunspots.

1900 A.D.

A.D. 1869 Cincinnati Red Stockings become first paid baseball players.

A.D. 1892 Hale invents the spectroheliograph.

A.D. 1868 George Ellery Hale born.

A.D. 1867 Mark Twain authors *The Jumping Frog.*

A.D. 1860 Warren de la Rue determines prominences are a solar feature.

A.D. 1861–1865 Civil War rages in the United States.

A.D. 1848–59 Sunspot cycle defined by Schwabe. Carrington witnesses first solar flare.

A.D. 1853 Alexander Wood uses hypodermic syringes for subcutaneous injections.

A.D. 1845 First photographs of the Sun.

A.D. 1776 U.S. Declaration of Independence.

A.D. 1814–15 Josef von Fraunhofer discovers dark lines in the solar spectrum.

A.D. 1726 Jonathan Swift writes *Gulliver's Travels.*

A.D. 1645 Beginning of the "Maunder Minimum."

A.D. 1612 Tobacco planted in the Virginia colonies.

A.D. 1610 Galileo observes the Sun with telescope.

A.D. 1592 Bubonic plague kills 15,000 in London.

1500 A.D.

A.D. 1350–1600 The Renaissance. Europe begins to emerge from the Dark Ages.

A.D. 1473 Copernicus born. His theories challenge Aristotle's.

A.D. 1271 Marco Polo travels to China.

A.D. 1052 Edward the Confessor begins building Westminster Abbey.

A.D. 1054 Brilliant supernova visible in daytime.

A.D. 950 Europe flounders in the "Dark Ages."

A.D. 963 *The Book of Fixed Stars* by Al Sufi mentions nebula.

A.D. 900–1300 Anasazi flourish in the American Southwest.

A.D. 79 Pompeii destroyed.

30 B.C. Antony and Cleopatra defeated.

A.D. 150–900 Mayans pursue astronomy and mathematics.

100 B.C. Gaius Julius Caesar born.

100 B.C.

336–339 B.C. Alexander the Great conquers Persia.

270 B.C. Aristarchus suggests the planets circle the Sun.

384 B.C. Aristotle born.

434 B.C. Anaxagoras suggests the Sun is a fiery stone.

776 B.C. First recorded Olympic games.

585 B.C. Thales of Miletus first predicts a solar eclipse.

1223 B.C. Syrian Tablet refers to solar eclipse

1555–1530 B.C. Amenhotep I reigns in Egypt.

2137 B.C. Old Chinese fable describes a solar eclipse.

2500 B.C. Egyptians begin to use papyrus for writing.

2800–1500 B.C. Stonehenge built, aligned to summer solstice sunrise.

2700 B.C. First Egyptian pyramids built

3150 B.C. Newgrange Tomb built; earliest known monument firmly linked to observations of the Sun.

3000–2500 B.C. Egyptians invade Palestine.

3150 B.C.

17

2
Scientific Development

During the last several centuries our knowledge of the Sun has progressed from an infancy nurtured in superstition and religious and political doctrine to an early adulthood that thrives on exploration and advancement. So many have contributed their genius to the ever-growing body of solar information that it is impossible to list their achievements. But let's highlight some of the milestones that brought us to the frontier of space-age astronomy.

Who were the modern forerunners of today's solar astronomers? Early on, during the 16th and 17th centuries, they came primarily from the ranks of doctors, mathematicians, inventors, and philosophers. By the 18th century they were men whose names we recognize, but not necessarily in connection with the Sun—Newton, Halley, and Herschel, to name just a few. A century later the new field of solar physics would begin to emerge, thanks largely to the work of men whose names are not as well known, but whose observations and innovative ideas taught us more in 100 years than we had learned in the previous millennium.

The heliocentric theory

From our perspective, the state of scientific awareness before the 18th century seems strange and remote. It is difficult to imagine being born into a world where the nature of the Sun itself is in question; where it is not realized that the twinkling points of light scattered throughout the nighttime skies are also suns. Moreover, these voids were filled by the creed of a powerful Church, or more accurately, Church-State, which refused to move from the ancient belief that the Earth was the center of the Universe, and the Sun pure and unblemished. Into this world however, came the son of a Polish merchant—Nicolaus Copernicus.

Copernicus was born in A.D. 1473, and went on to study both medicine and law. He became a skilled physician and then served for a time as an aide to his uncle, the Bishop of Varmia. Around 1510, Copernicus became interested in the workings of the solar system, not so much as a full-fledged astronomer, but more as a philosopher who thought the geocentric-Ptolemaic system was far too complex and probably inaccurate as well.

Breaking with a doctrine that had endured since Aristotle, Copernicus championed a Sun-centered, or heliocentric, system with the words, "And so, as if seated upon a royal throne, the Sun rules the family of the planets as they circle round him." Eventually, Copernicus successfully plotted planetary orbits. He understood that the Earth and Moon orbited the Sun between Venus and Mars and that Mercury was the innermost planet. However, Copernicus was not simply an astute scientist, he was also a political pragmatist; and when he published his earthshaking assertions in *De Revolutionibus* (1543), he also was shrewd enough to dedicate the controversial material to the current head of the Roman Catholic Church, Pope Paul III.

Why was the heliocentric theory so threatening? Perhaps the Church felt that if the heavens were truly infinite and Earth just one of many planets, human status would lose its uniqueness and the power of the Church could decline. Perhaps equally important from a religious point of view, a geocentric universe symbolized the centrality of humanity—of people who lived in a world, even a universe, created to fulfill their needs.

Much earlier, a school of Greek philosophers led by Aristarchus argued for a Sun-centered system similar to that promoted by Copernicus, but the earlier views of Plato and Aristotle had easily overcome that hypothesis. And since the Aristotelian point of view coincided with religious dogma, the medieval Church-State sealed the bargain by declaring other schools of thought to be heretical. In fact, the heliocentric theory became so threatening to the state that one of its more outspoken proponents, Giordano Bruno, was burned at the stake as a religious heretic. Small wonder the crafty Copernicus dedicated his work to a reigning Pope!

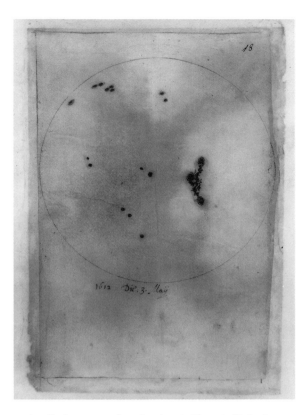

A detailed sunspot drawing by Galileo Galilei, circa 1611. *Photograph courtesy Biblioteca Apostolica Vaticana, Catalog Number 6479.*

Sunspots

The astronomical waters were still filled with dangerous shoals during the lifetime of Galileo Galilei, but friends in high places and brilliant work with the newly discovered telescope made both Galileo and his theories difficult to ignore. Then he turned from the Moon and planets to the curious dark specks that traversed the Sun's face, the forbidden imperfections of the Sun—sunspots. Although he wasn't the first to observe such features—Aristotle's own pupil, Theophrastus, made the first reliable report of a sunspot in the fourth century B.C., and the Chinese recorded what appear to be even earlier sunspot sightings on oracle bones hundreds of years beforehand—Galileo was one of the first to study them telescopically. Just two years after the invention of the telescope in

19

1608, he began three years of sunspot observation, eventually concluding that they were part of the solar landscape and not, as others had testified, small planets crossing the Sun's disk or even high-flying birds.

At about this time, the Jesuit priest Christopher Scheiner also began a lengthy period of solar observations. Naturally, Scheiner was strongly influenced by the Church, and as such became an arch-enemy of Galileo. At first he acquiesced to the prevailing belief that the spots were planets and used his observations to further the Aristotelian view of an unmarked Sun. When his theories were published anonymously, Galileo seized the opportunity to present his own ideas, partially as a defense of the Copernican theory. His rebuttal—and eventual destruction—of Scheiner's work through observation and empirical deduction was carried out in a series of letters written to Galileo's influential friend, Mark Welser, who published the letters in Rome.

During the years 1610 to 1613, Galileo observed that the spots moved across the Sun at a constant rate, and that their shapes were foreshortened as they neared the Sun's limb. To the intuitive Galileo, this meant the spots were rotating with the Sun and shattered the notion that they were not of solar origin. Eventually both Galileo and Scheiner realized that sunspots appeared mainly in circumsolar bands located within about 35 degrees of the equator; but Galileo went further, correctly concluding that the dark-looking regions were actually brighter than the Moon. Eventually, he would pay a high price for stating scientific truth, but Galileo's findings had already sounded the death knell for Aristotle's old theory of solar immutability and pointed to the truth of the Copernican theory.

And what of Scheiner? Although his interpretation of sunspots was shown to be incorrect—which he later acknowledged in a major concession to Galileo—his 16-year, well-documented series of sunspot observations proved invaluable years later when they were used to firmly establish the critical dates of at least one early sunspot cycle. And Scheiner's technique for observing the Sun safely, the method of projection, is popular even today.

Now, however, sunspot observers came up against a foe as formidable as the Church and belief in Aristotelian theory—the Sun itself. In a strange twist of fate, an almost total absence of spots on the Sun occurred from about 1645 to 1715. (Ironically, the lapse in spot appearance coincided with the reign of Louis XIV in France, known as the Sun King.) During the early part of the 20th century, this long lull would come to be known as the "Maunder Minimum" after E. W. Maunder, who, together with his wife Annie, compiled an extensive description of this seemingly unprecedented dearth of sunspots. But more about that later.

The laws of planetary motion

At the beginning of the 17th century, German astrologer and numerologist Johannes Kepler developed the basic laws of planetary motion, which determined the distances of the planets relative to one another. Briefly stated, he discovered that the planets moved around the Sun in elliptical rather than circular orbits, with the Sun at one focus of the ellipse; that a line (the radius vector) extended between Sun and planet sweeps over equal areas in equal times as the planet orbits the Sun; and that the squares of the periods of revolution of any two planets are proportional to the cubes of their mean distances from the Sun.

It is doubtful Kepler understood the actual cause of the laws of planetary motion; that was left to Isaac Newton, who believed Kepler had guessed at the first two and only grudgingly conceded him the third. However, some time after the end of the Maunder Minimum, the third, or harmonic law (Kepler's "music of the heavens") was combined with the passing of the planet Venus across the Sun's disk (a planetary transit) to permit the first realistic estimate of the distance between Sun and Earth since Hipparchus.

The procedure is simple. For example, the astronomer notes that the planet Venus never gets more than some 45 degrees from the Sun. The properties of a 45-degree triangle (in this case, formed by points represented by the Sun, Earth, and Venus) lead us to the conclusion that the distance of Venus from the Sun is about 0.7 that of the Earth. The relative distance of Mercury is similarly determined, and the outer planets are only slightly more complicated. A scale drawing is then made which includes all the planets at their relative distances from the Sun.

Now the problem is to determine the overall scale of the drawing. We can do this by learning the length of any line of the triangle. In 1716, Edmund Halley suggested that differences in Venus' track across the Sun could be measured from widely separated locations on the Earth, a measurement of the solar parallax. (Parallax is the apparent shift in position of an object due to a change in location of the observer.) The Venus transit of 1761 was observed in this manner, and in 1769 Captain James Cook sailed to New Zealand for the purpose of making observations to be compared with those from Europe. Measurement of the parallax through these techniques led directly to the Venus-Earth distance. Although the final result was delayed for several decades, the missing yardstick had been found and a solar distance to within a few percent of today's value was determined.

Sunspot cycles

In the year of the second transit, Scottish professor A. O. Wilson suggested that sunspots were shallow depressions in the solar surface and not, as had previously been believed, clouds, mountain peaks, or even solar volcanoes. Wilson believed the spots were part of a dark, solid solar core seen through openings in an outer covering. Surprisingly, some 20 years later the illustrious astronomer Sir William Herschel agreed with Wilson, stating that the Sun might well be "nothing else than a very eminent, large, and lucid planet." Furthermore, Herschel went on to explain that he believed the Sun was blanketed by two layers of clouds—a top covering which was highly luminous (the photosphere), and a bottom layer, which somehow protected the solar "inhabitants."

Unfortunately, Herschel's more dubious conclusions weren't limited to human citizens of the Sun. He also attempted to establish a connection between sunspots and wheat prices, initiating an apparently endless series of fruitless attempts to correlate sunspots with just about every conceivable earthly activity. Nearly all such efforts eventually prove to be examples of the well-known logical fallacy: *post hoc ergo propter hoc* (after A, therefore because of A!). Herschel theorized that

21

during times of increased sunspot activity the Sun's luminosity would decrease, and the resulting colder weather would reduce the wheat harvest. As farfetched as such a relationship appears, some modern studies have even attempted to correlate sunspot activity with outbreaks of the flu!

In the early 1800's the possibility of an intra-Mercurial planet was popular, and German amateur astronomer Heinrich Schwabe embarked on an observational program in which he kept an extensive record of daily sunspot activity. Although he never discovered the planet, Schwabe's records did reveal a cycle in the numbers of sunspots. In a paper published in 1843, he wrote, "From my earlier observations which I have reported every year in this journal, it appears that there is a certain periodicity in the appearance of sunspots, and this theory seems more and more probable from the results of this year." Schwabe's discovery went virtually unheeded until explorer Alexander von Humboldt included Schwabe's report in his monumental five volume work, *Kosmos*. Moreover, the timing of Schwabe's article happened to coincide with an analysis of data collected on terrestrial magnetism. When Edward Sabine informed the Royal Society of London that minima and maxima of the newly found sunspot cycle appeared to match that collected on magnetic variation, Schwabe's work suddenly gained much-deserved attention.

Prompted by this important breakthrough, Rudolf Wolf, then an astronomer at the Bern Observatory, reviewed sunspot data extending back to the observations of Galileo and confirmed Schwabe's findings; he noted, however, that the cycle was likely to be around 11 years in length, not 10, as proposed by Schwabe. During his search of the early records, Wolf recovered the long-lost notebooks of Danish astronomer Christian Horrebow, which showed that Horrebow had suggested a periodicity in the number of sunspots as early as 1776, a proposal which had been lost during the Napoleonic wars. Wolf went on to record sunspot activity for many years, during which time he developed a unique system for counting the groups of spots—the Universal, or relative, sunspot number, which is still in use today—and established a network of solar observing stations.

English amateur astronomer Richard Carrington was also intrigued by Schwabe's work, so much so that he turned his attention from plotting the positions of polar stars to tediously mapping the locations of sunspots and theorizing about their evolution. Using measurements obtained at his private observatory at Redhill, Carrington became the first to investigate the distribution of emerging sunspots during a solar cycle, noting that new cycle spots first appear at high latitudes and then slowly migrate toward the equator as the cycle runs its course. Later in the century, German astronomer Gustav Spörer compiled the first detailed analysis of this phenomenon, which has come to be called "Spörer's law."

The extremely productive Carrington also noticed that spots near the equator completed a rotation several days faster than those at higher latitudes, thus unearthing the concept of solar differential rotation. We do not know for certain if differential rotation is present deep within the Sun or is only a surface phenomenon. However, we do know that this feature is a consequence of the Sun's gaseous makeup, and some models of solar activity suggest that it generates the Sun's magnetic field by dynamo action.

Even though Carrington would shortly be required to put astronomy aside and spend his time running the family business, he made a final important contribution to our knowledge of the Sun. In so doing, Carrington laid the foundation for the study of the solar-terrestrial relationship. During one of Carrington's daily observing sessions he became the first to witness one of nature's most powerful phenomena—a blast of energy known as a "white-light" solar flare. In his report to the Royal Astronomical Society he wrote, "While engaged in the forenoon of Thursday, September 1 (1859), in taking my customary observation of the forms and positions of the solar spots, an appearance was witnessed which I believe to be exceedingly rare—two patches of intensely bright and white light broke out."

Over the next few minutes the patches "traversed a space of about 55,000 kilometers . . ." across the solar disk. In a second stroke of luck, Carrington's observation was independently confirmed by London astronomer Richard Hodgson, who stated, "the centre (of the light) might be compared to the dazzling brilliancy of the bright star, Beta Lyrae." Within a day a great geomagnetic storm ensued and was also duly noted: "The magnetic instruments at Kew were simultaneously disturbed to a great extent." Thus began the long supposed link between solar flares and geomagnetic storms.

Solar eclipse observation

While others continued their research in the day-to-day activities of the Sun, others, like the Englishman Francis Baily, turned their attention toward solar eclipses. Baily, a retired stockbroker turned amateur astronomer, traveled to Scotland to observe the 1836 eclipse. It was he who first noted "a row of lucid points, like a string of beads, irregular in size and distance from each other, (which) suddenly formed round that part of the circumference of the moon that was about to enter the Sun's disk," the effect called Baily's beads. Francis Baily was highly respected by his fellow astronomers. He was a founder of the Royal Astronomical Society, but spent his early days as an explorer. He was a meticulous record-keeper and kept a richly detailed journal of his 1796–97 travels through North America, in which he recounts the harsh winter of 1796, his Christmas Day loneliness, and an encounter in April 1797 with an old man "accompanied by his dog and his gun, and a few things lying at the bottom of the canoe"—Daniel Boone.

During the mid-19th century, a period of elaborately mounted eclipse expeditions began; several to the far-flung outposts that were still a part of the British Empire. And for the first time since the invention of the telescope, instruments were developed that enhanced solar observation and led directly to the understanding of some of its physical characteristics.

Over 100 observers took positions along the fortuitously located path of the 1842 eclipse, which ran through the densely populated area of southern Europe. For some reason not entirely certain, this eclipse was the first to prompt astronomers to seriously consider the true nature of solar prominences and the white mist surrounding the Sun and Moon at total eclipse, called the corona. There seemed to be no general agreement on the character of this nebulous

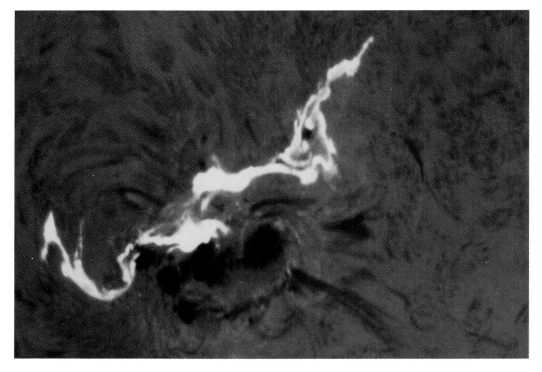

A brilliant solar flare, capable of being seen in white light, erupts above NOAA/USAF Region 5395 during March 1989. *Photograph courtesy of D.F. Neidig—Sacramento Peak Observatory.*

feature, but many believed that prominences were solar clouds or features of the Moon. Perhaps a man ahead of his time, Baily observed four large prominences during the 1842 eclipse and sketched them as if they emanated from the Sun's limb.

Solar photography and the nature of light

Soon after the invention of photography in 1845, Fizeau and Foucault made the first photograph of an astronomical object, the Sun. The first eclipse to be photographed passed through Europe in 1851. During this eclipse astronomers noted that prominences generally occurred near regions occupied by sunspots, but their exact nature was still a subject of controversy.

Nine years later the eclipse observations of Warren de la Rue settled the debate over whether prominences had a lunar or solar origin. He noted that the Moon moved relative to the prominences which appeared to be fixed to the Sun. The corona remained a mystery, although in 1872, writing in the journal *Nature*, French astronomer P. J. Janssen noted, "I observed the eclipse under an exceptional sky, and my observations lead me to assume a solar origin of the corona."

Now for a moment let's move back in time to the start of this incredible century. In 1802, nearly 150 years after Isaac Newton first discovered that sunlight could be broken into the primary colors by passing it through a prism, W. H. Wollaston reproduced Newton's experiment, but passed the incoming light through a narrow slit, observing, without magnification, several dark lines of unknown origin that appeared to separate the different colors.

A decade after Wollaston noted these features, a German optician named Josef von Fraunhofer made a discovery that would forever change the face of astronomy. In 1817 he wrote, "In the window-shutter of a darkened room I made a narrow opening . . . and allowed sunlight to fall on a prism. . . . I wished to see if in the color-image from sunlight there was a bright band similar to that observed in the color-image of lamplight. But instead I saw with the telescope an almost countless number of strong and weak vertical lines, which are, however, darker than the rest of the color image." Fraunhofer (for whom the series of lines is named) assigned letters of the alphabet to the more

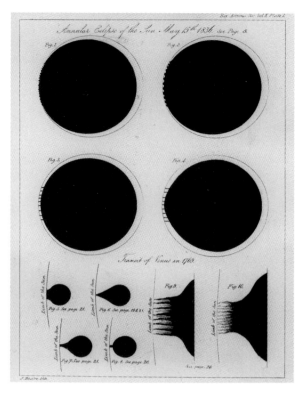

Sketches of Baily's beads and other solar phenomena by Francis Baily. *Photograph courtesy of P. D. Hingley, Librarian, the Royal Astronomical Society.*

conspicuous lines—he plotted over 500—beginning with the red portion of the spectrum (A), and moving to the violet (I). Naturally, the source of the lines immediately became a subject of intense debate. Were they caused by a freak telescopic defect, by Earth's atmosphere, or did they truly have a solar origin? For the next 30 years the scientific community pondered its interpretation of the Fraunhofer lines.

Then, at about the mid-point of the century chemist Robert Bunsen asked physicist Gustav Kirchhoff for help in developing a spectral analysis of the known chemical elements. While conducting a series of laboratory experiments in which such substances were exposed to heat, they discovered that by subjecting sodium salt to the flame of a Bunsen burner, a bright line (called an emission line) could be produced at the exact location of the dark Fraunhofer "D" line. Their work, *Chemical Analysis by Spectral Observations*, created an overnight sensation.

For the first time, scientists had a means to determine the composition of the Sun and other stars. Through spectral analysis—the interpretation of lines in the spectrum—the chemical composition of celestial bodies could be ascertained through information carried on light waves! Several decades later they would learn that magnetic fields could also be investigated through the splitting of such lines. From this point on, a great effort ensued; first Kirchhoff, later K. Angström and C. Thalén, and the American H. A. Rowland (Rowland employed a diffraction grating rather than prism), mapped thousands of lines in the solar spectrum.

After the 1851 eclipse it became obvious that valuable data could be collected by maintaining a daily photographic record of solar activity. In 1857, de la Rue designed a telescope—the photoheliograph—for the express purpose of making such records. Shortly thereafter the British Association for the Advancement of Science convinced de la Rue to transfer his instrument to the Kew Observatory and to direct a systematic observational program from that location. His instrument remained in daily use until the 1870's, when the work was assumed by the Royal Observatory at Greenwich, where it continued for over a century.

The Sun's elements

The solar eclipse that occurred in 1868 was the first to be observed spectroscopically. While undertaking these measurements, astronomers noted a bright spectral line that many took to be the Fraunhofer D-line. However, British astronomer Sir Norman Lockyer and P. J. Janssen independently discovered that the feature actually appeared at a slightly different wavelength. Scientists eventually found that the mysterious line was produced by a previously undiscovered element, helium, named for the Greek Sun god, Helios. Despite the relative lateness of its discovery, helium was found to be the second most abundant element—after hydrogen—in the universe. Nearly 30 years after its discovery on the Sun, helium was found on the Earth in association with the radioactive mineral uraninite. Another advance occurred during the 1868 eclipse. Lockyer reported, "after a number of failures . . . (succeeding in). . . obtaining and observing part of the spectrum of a solar prominence."

A year later P. J. Janssen captured the first photographs of the solar "granulation." Janssen's superb photographs and incredibly tedious techniques would not be bettered for nearly a century, and during the interim many explanations for granules would be put forward. The camera was later used to photograph coronal emission and the spectrum of the Sun's inner atmosphere, the chromosphere; and in 1898, H. H. Turner became the first to photograph light-polarization within the corona. A number of attempts were made to photograph prominences outside of eclipses but they would not be successful until the following century.

A flurry of scientific advances closed out the 19th century. But this was merely a prelude to the whirlwind of discovery that accompanied the onset of the 20th. And who better to carry such efforts forward than the larger-than-life persona of George Ellery Hale. Hale became interested in astronomy at around the age of 14. While he was attending MIT as an undergraduate, his wealthy father presented him with a spectroscopic laboratory. Hale began working on the unanswered questions connected with the nature of the solar spectrum and took up the challenge of photographing prominences outside of an eclipse.

Solar astronomy

In 1892, in the pursuit of his undergraduate thesis, Hale built an instrument that Janssen had first conceived in 1869. Based upon the familiar spectroscope, the new instrument—the spectroheliograph—could photograph solar features that radiated strongly within a particular line of the Sun's spectrum. Hale and French astronomer H. Deslandres both built instruments based on the same principle—a spectroscope with two adjustable slits that could isolate the light within a single spectral line. Hale's version, however, had the advantage of producing views of the Sun's disk in many wavelengths.

The young and dynamic Hale caught the public's imagination, as the following 1892 newspaper clip shows: "To be an able astronomer at twenty-four is something; to have acquired a special knowledge of a special subject in science that is rare even among scientific men is something more. . . . If the future of his work may be gathered from its past Professor Hale will certainly add more to the stock of human knowledge about the Sun than any other one man."

The photoheliograph designed by Warren de la Rue. De la Rue compiled the first extensive record of solar photographic observations with this instrument. *Photograph courtesy of P. D. Hingley, Librarian, the Royal Astronomical Society.*

In 1890 Hale had learned that the University of Southern California was to build the world's largest telescope using glass disks cast in France and polished into lenses by the famous Massachusetts lens-maker Alvan Clark and Sons. Shortly thereafter, the project was abandoned; Hale and others then persuaded transit magnate C. T. Yerkes to fund the huge refractor and locate it in Southern Wisconsin, where it could be operated by the University of Chicago.

After the Yerkes Observatory was completed, experimentation began using a horizontally mounted solar telescope, which Hale had designed. However Hale found both the solar telescope and climatic conditions at Yerkes to be unsuitable for such special work. Never at a loss for an idea, he turned his attention toward establishing a solar observatory in California, and eventually transported a version of the solar telescope (the Snow telescope) to the site. Thanks to a Carnegie grant, the Mount Wilson Solar Observatory was funded and rapidly became a center for studies in solar spectroscopy.

At Mount Wilson, Hale—learning that ground effects interfered with the horizontal telescope's image quality—changed course and designed a solar "tower"

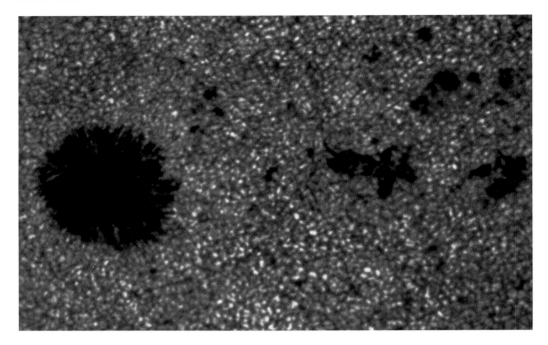

Solar granulation around a sunspot group. The photosphere can be resolved into a network of inter-locking small cells—the solar granulation. The granulation is a surface pattern of convective bub-bling that transports heat from inside the Sun to its surface. *Photograph courtesy of the National Solar Observatory/Sacramento Peak.*

telescope. A mirror (called a coelostat) was placed atop the tower where it directed sunlight down through a vertical tunnel and into a large spectrograph; this arrangement greatly reduced the destablizing air currents at ground level. With this instrument, and a second and taller tower telescope, he discovered that sunspots are magnetic in nature and that most are bipolar—their main leading and trailing spots have opposite magnetic polarities. Moreover, he noted that these polarities were reversed in the Sun's Northern and Southern Hemispheres. Then in 1913, as one solar cycle ended and another began, Hale observed an overall hemispherical reversal and became the first to describe and measure the Sun's 22-year magnetic cycle. All this information indicated the presence of a magnetic dynamo deep within the Sun that somehow generated these phenomena.

Hale resigned his position at Mount Wilson in 1923 because of ill health. In retirement, he built a private solar observatory where he invented the spectrohelioscope—a variation of the spectroheliograph that enabled visual observation. Soon afterward, he noted rapid changes in a type of extraordinarily bright, short-lived solar feature that had been recorded with spectroheliographs years before. Recognizing the importance of such events, Hale distributed spectrohelioscopes to several observatories and formed a network that monitored these "chromospheric eruptions." They were the phenomena that Carrington had first witnessed a half-century before—solar flares.

Along with his hands-on approach to scientific work, Hale was instrumental in forming the International Union for Co-operation in Solar Research (The Solar Union), a forum in which members of the global solar community could discuss ongoing research. In the meantime, Hale lobbied for a telescope even larger than the 2.5-meter Hooker on Mount Wilson, an effort which eventually resulted in the 5.1-meter aperture instrument located at Palomar Mountain that bears his name.

At the beginning of his career, the man who would come to be called the "father of solar physics" had written, "Some think that solar work is pretty well played out—in reality it is only just beginning. . . ." Hale may not have realized how prophetic his words were, but with his strong influence the field of solar physics was now firmly planted.

The work of Albert Einstein entered the astronomical picture on publication of his third famous paper in 1905. However, Einstein's worldwide fame really began over a decade later when one of the more arcane predictions of general relativity was tested and compared with a similar prediction by Isaac Newton: the bending of light as it passes near a strong gravitational field.

According to Newtonian mechanics, light from a distant star grazing the edge of the Sun is bent by 0.85 second of arc, whereas Einstein's general relativity predicts 1.7 seconds. The measurement of the doubling of this effect pitted an old established giant against a young, emerging one. The test took place at the May 1919 eclipse, and of course relativity won out. The result was acclaimed as one of the greatest scientific discoveries of modern times. Einstein received international recognition by the popular media as well as the scientific community and was on his way toward immortality.

Another leap forward in instrumentation occurred in 1930. French astronomer B. Lyot invented the first working coronagraph, a device that blocks the intense light from the solar disk and enables study to be made of the Sun's atmosphere outside of eclipse. With the instrument installed at the Pic du Midi Observatory in France, Lyot was able to secure the first non-eclipse photographs of the corona, and around 1936 he began using the coronagraph to photograph prominences. The noted lunar-planetary cinematographer and amateur astronomer R. R. McMath also began prominence photography around this time using the tower telescope located at the McMath-Hulbert Observatory in Michigan.

A few years earlier, McMath and his colleagues at the McMath-Hulbert Observatory pioneered the new field of taking motion pictures of the Sun. McMath employed the same principles as Hale used with the spectroheliograph, but speeded the process of picture-taking and projected the frames at a rate that allowed the eye to follow the relatively slow changes on the Sun. One of the most important applications of McMath's procedure dealt with prominences seen projected against the Sun (filaments). The graphic representations that resulted from McMath's process permitted detailed description and analysis of such features.

Legendary Harvard astronomer D. H. Menzel developed the first coronagraph in the United States in 1938. A year later he established the High Altitude Observatory at Climax, Colorado, an early U.S. solar observing outpost. From the turn of the century until World War II, unprecedented international cooperation and

The Swiss Federal Observatory in Zurich, Switzerland. From the inception of the sunspot number index until the end of 1980, the Swiss Federal Observatory served as the coordinating office for an international network of dedicated solar observers. The photograph shows how the facility and its surroundings looked in 1905. *Photograph courtesy of H. U. Keller.*

worldwide solar observation occurred. The Solar Union provided scientists with an opportunity to share information in such fields as solar radiation, sunspots, and spectroheliography. During that time the relationship between events on the Sun and those on the Earth became a subject of wide interest: fade-outs and other anomalies of the shortwave radio signal had been noted for years. Exactly what affect did the Sun have on the Earth's magnetic field and radio transmissions?

International cooperation slowed to a crawl along with most solar research at the outbreak of World War II. In Zurich, the *Quarterly Bulletin on Solar Activity* suspended publication. The Germans, isolated from most of the world's scientific community, built a solar observatory and a series of monitoring stations to forecast disturbances that might cause interference with shortwave radio transmissions and endanger the military communications network. Although many German scientists were involved in the destructive V-2 rocket program, some tried to use the new science of rocketry for research. In fact, they formulated a detailed plan that employed a V-2 rocket to carry an ultraviolet spectrograph aloft; but the war ended before the launch could take place.

Like the Germans, the Allies used the war years to monitor conditions affecting radio transmissions and other solar-related terrestrial phenomena. For the most part, the Allies maintained a sort of tenuous access to their existing pre-war facilities. Still, enough disruptions did occur that D. H. Menzel joined the fabled Harvard astrophysicist Harlow Shapley to instigate an American sunspot monitoring program administered by the American Association of Variable Star Observers and financed by the War Department. This program—now composed of a worldwide network of skilled observers—continues to supply the professional scientific community with valuable information about sunspots and flare effects on the ionosphere (see Appendix).

When World War II ended, M. Waldmeier resumed a full schedule at the Swiss Federal Observatory and once again instituted reports of solar activity. In the United States, instruments for successfully photographing the ultraviolet spectrum were launched above the ozone layer (the Sun's UV radiation is absorbed as ozone is created) aboard surplus V-2 rockets. Several years later, M. Schwarzschild used a balloon-borne experiment to obtain the first high-resolution photographs of the solar granulation since Janssen. This decade also saw H. D.

and H. W. Babcock map the location, polarity, and intensity of the Sun's magnetic fields with the aid of their newly invented magnetograph and develop a popular theory describing the solar dynamo.

Thereafter the solar community as a whole settled in for a period rich in funding. By 1953, 14 observatories were conducting visual solar observations and had coronagraphs; for the moment, Lyot's remained the largest of these instruments, still installed at Pic du Midi. At about this time, D. H. Menzel became a prime mover in the establishment of the National Solar Observatory at Sacramento Peak, located near the White Sands Proving Ground in New Mexico. In true American fashion, in the early 1950s work began on a 40-centimeter coronagraph, twice the size of Lyot's. After becoming director of Harvard College Observatory in 1954, Menzel was instrumental in building the Air Force-sponsored Solar Radio Observatory in Texas, which recorded radio waves of solar origin.

On the whole, solar astronomers enjoyed a period of postwar prosperity and looked forward to studies of the sunspot maximum expected to occur in 1957 or 1958. To coincide with the maximum, 1957 was chosen as the International Geophysical Year (IGY). While much valuable data was collected and many worthwhile programs begun, the IGY was somewhat overshadowed by a sudden event that changed the scope of scientific knowledge as surely as Copernicus' assertion of a Sun-centered Universe—Sputnik. How right Hale was.

A Reflected Sundial

We've seen how early humans kept track of the seasons, but how did they mark the hours of the day? Some measured time by the shadow of an upright stick driven onto the ground, others by a more elaborate system of shadows cast onto a surface marked with time intervals. These sundials are one of the earliest scientific instruments known. Sundials were used by the Egyptians as early as the 15th century B.C. and maintained their popularity well into A.D. 1800. The most common were known as "garden dials," many of which were richly adorned with phrases such as "I count only the hours that are serene." However, sundials have varied greatly in size, type, and layout. For example, in Jaipur, India, time was once read from the shadow cast by a stairway 36 meters long, and George Washington carried a hand-held dial that fit into his pocket.

Designs have run from the whimsical to the sublime. Sundials have been built to resemble bracelets, sextants, bird feeders, and even satellite dishes. One of the most interesting, however, is the "ceiling" or "reflected" dial. This type of sundial may have originated with Copernicus in the mid-16th century. And some say that Isaac Newton constructed a reflected dial on the ceiling of his grandmother's cottage. According to Rene Rohr, Vice-President of the British Sundial Society, the best known ceiling sundial was painted in 1673 on the walls and ceiling of a Jesuit residence in France.

Fred Sawyer and Robert Terwilliger of the North American Sundial Society (see Appendix) have been kind enough to supply us with the details of the reflected sundial design, described below.

Materials:

• A small first-surface mirror, 6 cm square (A first-surface mirror is silvered on its face rather than its back.)
• A roll of narrow masking tape and a pencil

Construction:

Begin by placing the small mirror on a window sill or another horizontal surface in a window where it will receive sunshine for a good part of the day. If the mirror is small enough, the image it reflects on the ceiling will be a circular spot of sunlight, even though the mirror itself is square.

If it is difficult to locate a mirror of that size, use a slightly larger one by covering it with a dark paper mask that contains an opening of the approximate size.

Generally speaking, the nearer the mirror is to the ceiling the better, because its reflection onto the ceiling will be seen for more of the day. If the mirror is too low, the reflected light spot will move quickly to the side and back walls of the room.

The simplest form of this experiment is to simply watch the daily motion of the reflected image of the Sun as it moves across your ceiling. In the summer when the Sun is high in the sky, the image will travel on a hyperbolic path from west to east, close to the window's wall. At the equinoxes the image follows a straight path across the ceiling. During the fall and winter the path becomes hyperbolic again, beginning at the

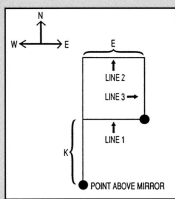

far west corner and moving closer to the window until midday, when it turns back on a path that carries it to the east. The extremes—closest to and farthest from the windows—occur at the summer and winter solstices, respectively.

The Sun appears to move across the sky at differing rates and therefore solar days vary in length. (Our clocks reflect the average solar day throughout the year.) The Sun is sometimes a little ahead and sometimes a little behind regular clock time. To see this effect, mark the location of the reflected solar image on the ceiling at the same time each day (ignore the consequences of Daylight Savings Time), and then connect the dots. If you continue this process for a full year, the result will be an analemma, a pattern in the shape of a figure 8. This design is seen on many old globes—often in the form of a strange-looking symbol placed somewhere in the Pacific Ocean. This feature is seldom mentioned today because most of us are unaware of its special significance.

If the Sun always moved at the same rate as our clocks, the analemma would collapse into a straight line. But when the Sun falls behind the clock during their annual race, the spot falls to the west of the line, and when the Sun pulls ahead, the spot appears to the east of the line. This east-west motion combines with the Sun's seasonal north-south travel in the sky to produce a symbol in the shape of a figure 8.

Creating a reflected dial that will show "solar time" requires a little mathematics—but only simple trigonometry functions, which are available on most modern scientific calculators.

Continue construction by tracing a true north-south line on the ceiling with narrow masking tape. (This procedure works for a horizontal ceiling; a cathedral-shaped ceiling is more complicated.) Do not use a magnetic compass to establish the line, since magnetic north and true celestial north are not the same. The simplest approach is to determine the time midway between sunrise and sunset for the day the line is drawn. Such information can be obtained from a local newspaper, television weather forecast or an almanac, but be certain the time is for your location.

At the appointed time, the reflected image will be exactly due north of the mirror's location. Mark that spot and establish a tape-line on the ceiling that extends from the spot to a point directly above the mirror. This line traces your meridian—the line of longitude running through your room.

Now lay out a complete rectangle on the ceiling with masking tape, using the north-south line as the western side of the rectangle. You will use these lines to locate afternoon hour-lines. Lines for the morning hours can be determined through a similar process, but with the rectangle drawn on the other side of the N-S line (that is, so that the N-S line forms its eastern boundary).

Refer to Figure 1 during the following steps, but bear in mind that you are looking at the drawing as if it is on the floor—and not as though it is over your head and you are looking toward the ceiling.

To find the sundial's hour-line for a particular time, say 2 P.M., proceed as follows:

Let H equal the height of the ceiling above the mirror (that is, the vertical distance between the ceiling and the surface holding the mirror), and K equal the distance of the east-west line of masking tape (Line 1 in Figure 1) from a point directly above the mirror.

For best results, draw the rectangle so that K is small; that is, establish this end of the rectangle so it is as close to the window

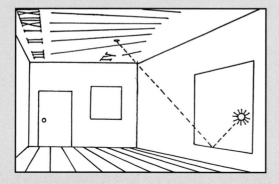

as possible.

Also, assign L the value of your latitude, and T the Sun's hour-angle (set the value of T at 15 degrees for each hour before or after noon; for example, 2 P.M. = 30 degrees).

Strictly speaking, this is the Sun's hour-angle for 2 P.M. local solar time. To get closer to the time our watches indicate, an additional adjustment for longitude would be required, but this does not appear in traditional sundials, nor is it something astronomers would have been particularly concerned about before the mid-19th or early 20th centuries.

Our hour-line for 2 P.M. will meet the east-west line (Line 1) at a distance P(1) from the N-S line, with

P(1) = tanT (K sinL + H cosL).

Of course, you will need two points to be able to draw the hour-line. If K* represents the distance from the ceiling point above the mirror to Line 2 (that is, the northernmost east-west-line of the rectangle), then the intersection of the hour-line with Line 2 occurs at distance P(2) from the N-S line, with

P(2) = tanT (K* sinL + H cosL).

Unfortunately, not all of the hour-lines will cross both Line 1 and Line 2, since the size of the rectangle is restricted by the confines of our ceiling. For these lines, you can locate the second point of the hour-line along Line 3 (the eastern N-S line of the rectangle).

In this case, let D represent the distance between the original N-S (west) line of the point of rectangle and Line 3. The distance P(2*) of the point of intersection from the southeast corner of the rectangle measured along Line 3 is determined according to

$$P(2^*) = \frac{D \cot T - H \cos L}{\sin L} - K.$$

(Positive values lie to the north, negative to the south.)

Once you've found two points to establish an hour-line, you can draw a straight line with tape that connects them. Extend the line in both directions (toward and away from the window) and you have another hour-line for the sundial. Continue in this way for other hour-lines.

Remember, however, that the lines will not match clock time. If you wanted them to be the same, you would require a series of figure 8's drawn on the ceiling. Instead, you have reproduced a traditional sundial, which indicates solar time. If you would like to convert a reading to clock time, try one of the following.

1. Read the material on sundials published annually in the *Old Farmer's Almanac*. This publication provides a column containing an adjustment procedure for every day of the year that gives the time—faster or slower—of the Sun compared with the clock.

2. Refer to your local newspaper or weather broadcast and determine the time exactly halfway between sunrise and sunset. The sundial will read (solar) noon at this time. The difference between solar noon and local noon can be used throughout the day to adjust for "Sun-fast" or "Sun-slow," conditions, but remember that this adjustment slowly changes from day to day.

3

Space Age Solar Astronomy

On an October evening in 1957 the world was turned upside down; a Soviet R-7 rocket blasted off from the Baikonur Cosmodrome carrying a beach-ball-sized satellite called Sputnik. For the next few months it circled the globe, its radio transmitter signaling what U.S. Senator Henry Jackson called "a devastating blow to the prestige of the United States as the leader of the scientific and technical world." By one dramatic act, the Soviet Union both deflated U.S. national pride and prodded it out of complacency. America was caught flat-footed as the space age dawned.

Playing catch-up wasn't easy. Two months later, the Navy's ill-fated attempt to gain the high ground resulted in a launch pad explosion, which pundits dubbed "kaputnik." A second attempt resulted in yet another failure. Public and political pressure mounted. Finally, on January 31, 1958, an Army Jupiter-C rocket roared into space carrying Explorer 1, designed by James Van Allen of the Jet Propulsion Laboratory in Pasadena, California. The satellite achieved orbit, and the young space age gave birth to the space race.

Now, no longer confined to Earth-based exploration, scientists turned their attention to new vistas. Sputnik and Explorer freed astronomers, at least theoretically, to sail their 20th-century ships through the previously uncharted realm of space. Confidently, sights were set on the future. . . . and what a future it would be. Redstone, Atlas, Mercury, Gemini—all precursors to the greatest show on Earth— a manned mission to the Moon. But while the world watched spacewalks and docking maneuvers, a group of astronomers quietly geared up for a different race; one that would use this exciting new technology to investigate our own cosmic neighborhood as never before possible. And while some turned their eyes to the planets, others set their sights on the star at the center of our solar system—the Sun.

Pioneer 4 gained distinction as the first manmade object to orbit the Sun, but it was just one of many workhorse spacecraft to follow. Pioneer successfully gathered radiation and other solar data from its unique location in space. The space probe was followed a year later by Pioneer 5, which monitored solar flares. Meanwhile, as U.S. astronauts took a positive step forward with Marine Colonel John

Glenn's orbital flight, solar astronomers were on their way to a new understanding of the physics of the Sun.

Solar wind

Fast on the heels of Pioneer, Mariner 2 verified the presence of a plasma that continuously flows away from the Sun—the solar wind—and instruments aboard the Explorer 18 Interplanetary Monitoring Platform detected the shock-wave produced when the wind collided with Earth's magnetosphere. Explorer 30 sensors monitored solar X-rays, measurable only from outside the Earth's protective atmosphere, at about the same time that astronauts Gus Grissom and John Young practiced orbital changes in the Gemini spacecraft.

During this heady period, the terrestrial effects of solar activity began to be investigated with special satellites that monitored the near-Earth environment. The High Eccentric Orbit Satellite examined interactions between Earth's magnetosphere and energetic solar particles, Explorers 6 and 10 observed terrestrial electric fields and the magnetosphere, and Explorer 50 monitored the Earth's magnetotail (the portion of the magnetosphere that trails the Earth through space) and the middle field of radiation between the Earth and Moon. Slowly but surely, the secrets of the relationship between the Sun and Earth began to be unraveled.

While the world's eyes were focused on a gigantic Saturn rocket and Apollo 8's historic circumlunar voyage, one of the most productive spacecraft of all time was making a little history of its own. Pioneer 9, launched in November 1968, provided scientists with detailed measurements of the solar wind, the Sun's magnetic fields, and cosmic rays. Previously, astronomers thought the solar wind meandered through interplanetary space like a lazy river, but Pioneer 9 proved otherwise. In reality the gentle stream was more like a raging river, mercilessly plowing through space at a million kilometers per hour. The Sun was not a quiet star!

With an avid audience that included, among others, the Federal Aviation Administration, the military, and civilian power and communication companies, Pioneer 9 kept its watchful eye on the Sun, continuously recording new information but also looking for potential trouble spots. And since unexpected large bursts of solar radiation could adversely affect astronauts in translunar orbit, hourly reports of solar activity from Pioneer were sent to Mission Control during the Apollo flights. Then in 1972—the year of the last manned U.S. Moon mission—while Earth was being battered by a great solar storm, Pioneer 9 and its sister ship, Pioneer 10 (then on its way to the planet Jupiter), were positioned to measure the solar wind from both upstream and downstream locations.

The data acquired by Pioneer provided evidence that the outward-rushing gases that make up the solar wind lose speed but increase in temperature as they move through space, demonstrating that a portion of the wind's motion is converted to thermal energy. Pioneer 9 was designed to last only a few months, but the craft continued to send signals back to Earth until 1983, when its acquisition of scientific data gathered during 22 solar orbits finally ended after sending over 4000 million bits of data back to Earth.

Even today Pioneer 10 continues to seek out information about the heliopause, the region in space where the Sun's expanding atmosphere merges with interstellar space. Once we believed the heliosphere ended near the outer reaches of the solar system, but instruments on board Pioneer (and more recently, the Voyager spacecraft) have demonstrated that the Sun's influence is felt at a much greater distance (see Chapter 4). Although Pioneer 10 is now more than 8000 million kilometers away, it continues to send important data back to Earth. Physicist James Van Allen has referred to Pioneer 10 and its sister ship, Pioneer 11, as "two of the great scientific successes of the space age." Van Allen notes that Pioneer may leave the heliosphere and enter interstellar space before contact is lost with the spacecraft around the year 2000.

Orbiting observatories

The first United States space station, Skylab, was launched on May 14, 1973. It carried eight telescopes within its Apollo Telescope Mount. Five were used to observe the Sun in X-ray and ultra-violet wavelengths, one was used as a coronagraph, and two were employed to televise solar images to the crew so they could keep track of likely observing targets such as strong flares. During one extraordinary day, 31 separate flares were recorded.

Edward Gibson, a solar physicist and author of *The Quiet Sun,* was aboard the third and last of Skylab's missions. As an astronaut, one of Dr. Gibson's fondest hopes was to capture the "moment of birth" of a solar flare. Just one week before the mission's end Gibson's persistence paid off. After monitoring a large active sunspot region for many days, Gibson noticed a rapidly brightening area on the Sun—a flare on the rise—and was able to realize his wish by documenting the event on film.

Eventually the Skylab crews compiled a photographic record of the Sun like none before, averaging nearly 600 images per day. The first flare photograph from space was taken by one of its teams, and the Skylab coronagraph operated successfully for over eight months. Before Skylab the entire history of solar photography had resulted in less than 80 hours of information from eclipses.

Advanced observing equipment

The Vacuum Telescope at Kitt Peak, Arizona, was one of the many ground-based instruments built to support Skylab's work. Chosen for its high degree of sky transparency—a measurement of how free the atmosphere is from smoke, dust, and water vapor—the Kitt Peak site remains sacred to the nearby Papago Indians. The "people with the long eyes" (astronomers) currently operate 22 telescopes at Kitt Peak National Observatory, including the vacuum telescope, a coelostat-fed 76-centimeter reflector with a 36-meter focal length designed by Dr. William Livingston of the National Solar Observatory.

The telescope began operation in 1972, but continues in active use long after Skylab's demise. Among other projects, the instrument currently collects daily full-disk, 1-arc-second-per-pixel solar magnetic maps, full-disk helium spectroheliograms, and images taken in the calcium band of the solar spectrum. Each month, information obtained with the Vacuum Telescope is processed into special solar rotation maps and distributed to the Space Environment Services and the World Data Center in Boulder, Colorado, to be made available to researchers. Observations compiled during this project have provided astronomers with a detailed 20-year record of solar magnetic activity.

Several diverse programs are currently underway at Kitt Peak National Solar Observatory. The High-Resolution Infrared Spectroscopy of the Carbon Monoxide Molecule project is one such experiment. Carbon monoxide (CO) in the solar atmosphere is thought to exist primarily in highly structured and anomalously cool clouds in the high photosphere and low chromosphere. The temperature in these structures can be as low as -3700 Kelvin, significantly cooler than the average photospheric temperature of ≈6000 degrees.

Several explanations have been proposed for this apparent thermal bifurcation. For example, radiative cooling by CO itself may trigger a thermal instability. Alternatively, the dominant effect may be the quasi-adiabatic cooling of gas lofted into the mid-photosphere by the overshoot of granular convection. If several mechanisms are at work, their relative importance is probably modulated by the presence of concentrated magnetic fields. Astronomers want to understand where, when, and why CO exists in order to understand how the solar photosphere departs from simple one-dimensional models in hydrostatic equilibrium and how this complex structure is related to the existence of the chromosphere.

During 1993–1994, two infrared experiments at the 1.5-meter McMath-Pierce Telescope—the largest solar telescope in the world—probed the spatial and temporal distribution of CO in the atmosphere. One team used the McMath 13.7-meter vertical spectrograph and an infrared array camera to obtain high-resolution spectra of more than a dozen CO lines during the partial phases of the annular solar eclipse of May 10, 1994. It is particularly difficult to study the vertical distribution of CO because the layer in which it forms is extraordinarily thin (only about 1 arc second). Eclipse observations can use the distant "knife-edge" of the advancing lunar limb to achieve an effective angular resolution of about 0.1 arc second, ten times better than is possible with conventional observations degraded by atmospheric turbulence and telescope diffraction. Initial analysis of these data reveals that emission from some spectral lines extends significantly less than has been inferred from existing non-eclipse data, a finding that will require modifications to the models previously proposed to interpret those observations.

Another team exploited the imaging capability of the infrared array camera to analyze spatially and temporally resolved CO spectra in active and quiet regions on the solar disk. The observations show that, in the quiet Sun, spatial variations in CO intensity are largely dynamical, supporting the theoretical suggestion that dynamical effects play a key role in the formation of the dark CO line cores.

The He 10830+ Video Filtergraph / Magnetograph, a new instrument for high spatial and temporal resolution imaging of solar active regions and flares in the 10830+ line of Helium is being developed under the Memorandum of Agreement between AURA and NASA's Goddard space flight Center (GSFC) for use at the Kitt Peak Vacuum Telescope (KPVT). The instrument will simultaneously observe with the spectromagnetograph. Nearly two decades of full-disk observations in the 10830+ line at the KPVT show a wide range of solar phenomena such as coronal holes, filament channels associated with coronal mass ejections, long-duration flares, and analogs to X-Ray bright points which are otherwise viewed on the disk only from spacecraft.

The filtergraph will provide a new view of transient phenomena in solar active regions with temporal and spatial resolution which cannot be observed from the spectromagnetograph, where data images are built by scanning the telescope's solar image across a long entrance slit. The new data will be particularly timely for comparisons with observations from the SOHO spacecraft, which promise to resolve long-standing controversies on how the formation of the line depends upon eternal EUV radiation from the corona and low-temperature transition region.

The instrument is built around a cleverly packaged five-element Lyot filter. Ferroelectric liquid crystals modulate bandpass response and polarization at video rates. Subtracting accumulated observations in three possible pairs of filter transmission modes provides active-region imagery of 10830+ equivalent width, line-of-sight velocity, or longitudinal magnetic field with time cadence of a few seconds. J. Harvey provided the basic concept and optical design, NASA/GSFC the detailed design and drawings, and the instrument was fabricated in NOAO shops using calcite birefringent crystals obtained from the GONG project.

By the end of 1994, the filter had been tested and tuned, the optical assembly installed in the KPVT, and satisfactory video images obtained with the filter in its four-element, centrally tuned mode. All hardware for the filtergraph and its data system are on hand and the basic software for differential accumulation of images has been written and tested. In the near future, the liquid crystal modulators will be installed, the data system connected, demonstration data obtained, and the development of a graphical user interface for routine control should be underway.

Not all programs are conducted at the observatory site itself. The South Pole '94 Helioseismology project, a joint effort between Bartol Research Institute, NASA and NSO started in 1993. The goal is to make solar oscillation observations from the geographic South Pole during the 1994–1995 austral summer. The observations will complement those from GONG (see below) and the Solar Oscillations Imager to be launched on the SOHO spacecraft. Unlike previous observations, the new ones will concentrate on high-frequency oscillations measured simultaneously at two heights in the solar atmosphere.

This project will glean information about the solar interior, and provide unique data about how waves propagate in the solar atmosphere. Instrument testing in summer 1994, showed that certain oscillation frequencies of the atmosphere are unusually sensitive to the amount of solar activity. In addition, newly erupting magnetic flux and about-to-erupt solar filaments are easily seen in the observations—information that will be invaluable to forecasters and solar scientists.

Unmanned orbiting observatories

After the Skylab project ended, the Sun's corona and magnetic field were monitored by the Helios spacecraft, conducted by the United States and West

Germany. Helios moved to an orbit that took it within about 46 million kilometers of its target. Shortly thereafter, several new satellites were commissioned to gather more data on the solar-terrestrial relationship. The Japanese spacecraft, SRATA (Solar Radiation and Thermospheric Structure) observed the conflict between solar wind particles and Earth's magnetosphere, while the International Sun-Earth Explorer 2 (ISEE-2) observed the interaction between emissions from the Sun and the terrestrial environment at the edges of the Earth's magnetic field.

Other important U.S. spacecraft included Nimbus 7, a primary weather satellite and the first spacecraft built to monitor Earth's atmosphere for artificial and natural pollutants. NASA's Total Ozone Mapping Spectrometer (TOMS) aboard the Nimbus 7 satellite measured Antarctic ozone levels from November 1978 to May 1993. During its lifetime on Nimbus 7, TOMS made ozone a household word through pictures of the Antarctic ozone hole. TOMS data also provided part of the scientific underpinning for the Montreal Protocol, under which many of the world's developing nations have agreed to phase out the use of ozone-depleting chemicals.

Another satellite, ISEE 3, was sent aloft to study coronal mass ejections and their effect on geomagnetic disturbances. In 1978, ISEE 3's name was changed to International Comet Explorer (ICE) when it was sent to study Comet Giacobini-Zinner and later Comet Halley. Among other important findings, during the solar portion of its mission ISEE 3's instruments uncovered a transient five-month periodicity in the frequency of solar flares, which aided in the search to unlock the secrets of these powerful events.

The initial space-based solar observations of the 1960s and 1970s yielded a wealth of information that was previously suspected but unsubstantiated. However, the Valentine's Day launch in 1980—near the peak of solar cycle 21—of the Solar Maximum Mission satellite ("Solar Max") enabled the solar physics community to verify many of their previous conclusions, while examining some of the most violent aspects of solar activity in greater detail than ever before.

By the time Solar Max was launched, the solar community had thoroughly digested most of the information unearthed by Skylab. While providing answers to many existing problems the findings also posed a number of new questions, and Solar Max was designed to provide the answers. Did flares have systematic precursors? What is the physical mechanism underlying the release of energy in a solar flare? Does the total solar energy output (irradiance) vary with the solar activity cycle? And how much energy is radiated at various wavelengths during a typical flare? A cooperative team composed of scientists from many parts of the world was established to gather and analyze the data that hopefully would provide clues to the answers of such questions.

Indeed, just three months after launch a fortuitous circumstance occurred on the Sun. Instruments aboard the satellite were able to carefully document, in minute detail, a giant flare that enveloped more than 6000 million square kilometers—enough to cover the surface of Jupiter. In addition to this stunning achievement, during its relatively short time in space Solar Max compiled a large bank of data on the corona and solar magnetic fields. But then, to the dismay of solar astronomers throughout the world, a failed attitude control system put the satellite abruptly out of commission.

Fortunately, several years later astronauts successfully repaired the ailing satellite and it resumed its rapid pace of discovery. Its measurements of the solar irradiance enabled astronomers to learn that it did, in fact, vary with the solar cycle, and that small decreases in the irradiance occurred when large sunspot groups passed across the Sun's disk. Moreover, for the first time astronomers were able to study flares through observations in all portions of the electromagnetic spectrum. According to researchers at the Goddard Space Center, the view through each "slice" contributed a different piece of the puzzle associated with the development of a solar flare: the way flares form, the conditions that precede them, and what happens as a flaring region returns to its quiet state.

It now became possible to locate and measure the source of "hard" X-rays (highly energetic forms of X-rays) produced in some flares. Researchers showed that these emissions occurred at a much earlier stage of a flare's development than previously thought. Additional findings rebutted the long-held belief that X-rays emanated from the top of the magnetic arch as a flare erupts, showing instead that they are rooted in the bases, or "footpoints," of the magnetic field.

Although it was designed to operate for only two years, Solar Max was able to function for ten. In all, the satellite obtained over 12,000 flare photographs, discovered ten Sun-grazing comets, and transmitted 250,000 images of the corona—100,000 in ultra-violet light. Among these were images that verified and detailed the apparent differences in the Sun's corona at sunspot maximum and minimum (long noted by ground-based observers), and spectacular renderings that outlined zones of differing density within the Sun's expanding atmosphere.

Lamentably, the object of the spacecraft's detailed observations also put an end to the magnificent performance of the Solar Maximum Mission. An unexpected large increase in solar activity caused enough atmospheric drag to pull Solar Max from orbit prematurely. NASA did not send a second rescue mission, and on December 2, 1989, the Solar Maximum Mission spacecraft re-entered Earth's atmosphere and disintegrated over the Indian Ocean.

Compilation of X-ray imaging begun by Solar Max was carried into the 1990s by Solar A, a joint project of Japan, the U.S., and England. Solar A was launched from Kagoshima Space Center in Japan and was later renamed "Yohkoh" (Japanese for sunbeam or sunlight). Yohkoh's primary goal is to provide detailed information about the structure of the corona and solar flares. The satellite's Hard X-Ray Telescope is designed to help astronomers learn more about how and where such X-rays are emitted in the magnetic loops accompanying flares, while its Soft X-Ray Telescope continually captures data on the corona.

Among others, the information from Yohkoh and other satellites is supplied to the International Ursigram and World Days Service (IUWDS), an organization established to disseminate information to the worldwide solar community. Yohkoh's daily X-ray images of the Sun's atmosphere help forecasters predict solar-terrestrial disturbances by monitoring the size, movement, and location of the low-density areas in the corona we call coronal holes.

Solar radiation monitors

The IUWDS operates several Regional Warning Centers (RWCs) around the world. Information concerning the Sun-Earth environment is collected by the RWCs and distributed daily as "Geoalert" bulletins. Each center prepares an individual forecast that is sent to the World Warning Agency in Boulder, Colorado. IUWDS clients include not only the solar astronomy community, but also radio communications and satellite operators, commercial mining and pipeline companies, power utilities, and the military—all of which can be directly affected by bursts of solar radiation.

Additionally, the IUWDS sponsors Solar Terrestrial Prediction Workshops to further the science of solar activity forecasting. Similarly, the Hiraiso Solar Terrestrial Research Center in Ibaraki, Japan, issues alerts of solar eruptions and geomagnetic storms, and Japan's Communications Research Laboratory is developing a Space Weather Forecast network. The rapid growth of sophisticated technology that can be influenced by events on the Sun has vastly increased the need for accurate solar-terrestrial forecasts.

As you might expect, very special instruments and techniques are required to study such phenomena. Geotail, a Japanese-American satellite, was launched during July 1992 to study precisely how the Sun affects Earth's magnetosphere. In order to observe the composition and activity of both the near and far magnetotail, Geotail was initially placed into a highly elliptical orbit measuring approximately 53,000 x 1.5 million kilometers; it was then moved closer to the Earth in a more nearly circular orbit.

According to the National Aeronautics and Space Administration, Geotail "travels into the magnetic tail of the magnetosphere on the night side of Earth—an area that is critical to understanding the interaction between the Sun and Earth." Geotail is the first craft to fully explore this region of the terrestrial environment. It is hoped that observations from this unique location in space will help determine the structure of Earth's magnetotail and increase our knowledge of the variations that occur as the tail interacts with the solar wind. Geotail will be followed by future launches of NASA's Solar and Heliospheric Observatory and the four-spacecraft Plasma Turbulence Laboratory mission, in collaboration with the European Space Agency.

Predictably, a number of exciting discoveries emerged from these and similar studies. In 1993 the Solar Anomalous and Magnetospheric Particle Explorer (SAMPEX), a combined effort of the U.S. and Germany, began to determine the precise composition of energetic particles arriving at Earth from the solar atmosphere and interstellar space. Thus far, SAMPEX has uncovered an additional radiation belt surrounding the Earth, partly composed of anomalous cosmic rays. In keeping with the current trend toward investigations directly related to activities on the Earth, SAMPEX is also designed to monitor fast electrons and the part they play in the chemical reactions leading to the formation and depletion of ozone in our atmosphere.

Taking a closer look

One of the more striking attempts to learn the secrets of the Sun occurred in 1990, when a vehicle was launched to study solar regions never before seen—the Sun's polar regions. Carried aloft by the Space Shuttle *Discovery*, this unique spacecraft was routed the long way around—by way of Jupiter. A joint undertaking between NASA and the European Space Agency, the project was initially called the "International Solar Polar Mission," but in 1984 its name was appropriately changed to Ulysses, the hero of Greek mythology who voyaged into the unknown.

After launch Ulysses sped toward Jupiter at speeds upwards of 15 kilometers a second, arriving in its vicinity during 1992. Why away from the Sun and toward Jupiter? Modern launch vehicles simply do not have the necessary thrust to propel a spacecraft up and out of the ecliptic plane (the plane of Earth's orbit around the Sun). Just such a trajectory was necessary for Ulysses, since its main mission is to circle the Sun's poles. When Ulysses reached the neighborhood of the huge

This illustration shows the Ulysses spacecraft as it begins its pass below the Sun's south pole. Ulysses reached 70 degrees south of the Sun's equator on June 26, 1994, and began to study previously unexplored regions. Photograph courtesy of the Jet Propulsion Laboratory — California Institute of Technology/NASA.

planet, Jupiter's considerable gravity seized the tiny craft, swinging it around the planet and back toward the center of the solar system and its rendezvous with the Sun.

In mid-1994 Ulysses completed its journey of nearly 2000 million kilometers, finally soaring over the Sun's South Pole, where it spent four months gathering data. Ulysses then set its sights on the opposite polar region, where it arrived during the summer of 1995. Although Ulysses was designed to study the Sun it-self, the project has already obtained new information about the heliosphere, the effects of the solar wind on Jupiter's magnetosphere, and the origins of cosmic dust. (Cosmic dust appears to stem from several sources: interstellar space, collisions within the asteroid belt, and remnants left over from the creation of the solar system.)

Ulysses carries special equipment designed to evaluate the total solar environment. It makes measurements of the solar wind, X-rays, and gamma radiation; and a search is underway for evidence of the gravitational waves predicted by Albert Einstein. With the aid of two sophisticated magnetometers, a three-dimensional map will be created of the Sun's looping magnetic fields, which extend far into the space surrounding the Sun. Perhaps most important, while flying above the poles, Ulysses is able to study the solar wind and coronal holes from a unique vantage point.

According to E. J. Smith of the Jet Propulsion Laboratory, "We have been like explorers confined to travel near the Earth's equator without being able to journey to the Arctic regions. For a long time, we have suspected that much of the solar phenomena studied at, and near, the Earth was controlled by conditions in the Sun's polar regions, but never before have we been able to observe these processes." Now, with Ulysses' successful flight above the poles, these previously inaccessible areas are about to yield their secrets to direct measurement.

As 1994 comes to a close, Ulysses has completed its exploration of the regions surrounding the Sun's South Pole, providing scientists with their first opportunity to obtain measurements directly from a location never before visited by spacecraft or ground-based instruments. Now that Ulysses is moving toward the solar equator and into the Sun-Earth region where the spacecraft's axial boom is illuminated by the Sun, it is monitored on a 24-hour basis by the European Space Agency's tracking facility at Kourou, French Guiana, and by NASA's Deep Space Network facility at Canberra, Australia.

The solar atmosphere

While Ulysses continues its mission, another type of solar mystery—the physical mechanism involved in the formation, structure, and eventual expulsion of solar filaments, is under scrutiny at an important ground-based facility. Sara Martin of the California Institute of Technology's Big Bear Solar Observatory is the Principal Investigator of a three-year project that will analyze these phenomena in greater detail than possible in earlier studies.

Martin's research, in which soft X-ray data from the Yohkoh satellite are correlated with magnetic field data and hydrogen-alpha images, deals with the mechanics and forces at work in the magnetic field configurations of filaments and in the channels where they are formed. Thus far, she has learned that there are two classes of magnetic field configuration for filament channels and filaments related to the way concentrations of opposite polarity magnetic flux behave. The two types are called dextral and sinistral.

She has also distinguished two structural classes of prominences. These are designated by the direction of the appendages of prominences relative to the major axis, and are named right-bearing and left-bearing. A one-to-one correspondence occurs between the magnetic and structural classes: dextral filaments are right-bearing, and sinistral are left-bearing.

Moreover, Martin has unearthed a pattern—apparently independent of the solar cycle—wherein dextral filaments dominate in the Northern Hemisphere and sinistral govern in the south. However, it is still not clear how all of the physical processes at work in the formation of filaments and prominences operate, or how the hemispheric pattern is related to the Sun's global magnetic field.

In addition to a number of other research studies, ongoing programs at Big Bear Solar Observatory include analyses of the dynamics of solar flares, investigations of the evolution of complex solar regions, and evaluation of the magnetic fields of active regions and the quiet Sun.

Since the early 17th century astronomers have observed the solar surface and atmosphere. But are there ways to investigate the interior workings of the Sun? The answer is yes. A network of solar scientists, the Global Oscillation Network Group (GONG) was formed in 1984 to conduct a detailed study of the Sun's structure through a new branch of solar physics called helioseismology—the study of sound waves that propagate through the Sun's interior. By examining such vibrations, researchers can make measurements of the internal structure and dynamics of the Sun.

The waves, which manifest themselves as oscillations at the solar surface, were discovered in the 1960s, and were first thought to be chaotic in nature. However, a major 5-minute oscillation appeared, during which the Sun seemed to undergo mechanical pulsations; eventually the vibrations were determined to be systematic. The GONG network will constantly monitor the "ringing" produced by the Sun's many modes of oscillation through a world-wide six-station network outfitted with sensitive solar velocity imagers.

At peak efficiency, each of these stations is expected to acquire over 200 megabytes of data per day, which will then be analyzed and released to the scientific community. In order to avoid discontinuities in the data flow imposed by nightfall, the network will be composed of member stations strategically located throughout the world. Monitors will operate at the Big Bear Solar Observatory (California), Learmonth Solar Observatory (Australia), Udaipur Solar Observatory (India), Observatorio del Teide (Canary Islands), Cerro Tololo Inter-American Observatory (Chile) and Mauna Loa Observatory (Hawaii). Initial site surveys have determined that this network will provide better than a 93 percent coverage of the Sun. Data acquisition is scheduled to run for a minimum of three years, with an added year of full-scale analysis.

More eyes on the Sun

Another ground-based platform for solar research is centered at the National Solar Observatory at Sacramento Peak, near Sunspot, New Mexico. At an altitude of 2800 meters, the site was picked for its dry air and distance from any major source of air pollution. The Vacuum Tower Telescope at the observatory collects sunlight with mirrors mounted on a concrete pier that rises approximately 40 meters above the ground. Its height helps to avoid ground-level atmospheric turbulence, which contributes to the motion and blurring of the image of the Sun. The telescope extends over 65 meters beneath the ground. The image itself is formed at ground level, where it can be studied by a variety of equipment.

As with the Vacuum Telescope at Kitt Peak National Observatory, the main tube is evacuated of all air which could affect the image; hence the name "vacuum tower" telescope. The entire telescope rotates during the day to follow features on the Sun. In spite of the occasionally poor seeing conditions associated with a desert mountain site, the Vacuum Tower Telescope has been called one of the finest solar telescopes in the world. The instrument is theoretically able to detect size differences of only 0.25 second of arc, equivalent to reading a license plate 100 kilometers away.

The John W. Evans solar facility at Sacramento Peak houses a single steel optical bench known as a "spar," which tracks the Sun each day. A variety of instruments can be mounted on the spar, but the main telescope at the Evans facility is a coronagraph. Since the solar atmosphere is a million times fainter than the surface of the Sun, dust and scratches on the coronagraph lenses must be carefully removed to avoid scattered light. (Until recently, only lenses could be used in coronagraphs, but now with a new super-polishing technology, coronagraphs can also be made with reflecting mirrors.)

The Hilltop Dome at Sacramento Peak Observatory also contains an instrument array mounted on a tracking spar. The Hilltop Dome facility is especially suited to experimental instruments, such as a reflecting solar coronagraph and a special magnetograph designed to study the magnetic fields associated with solar active regions. A final Sacramento Peak facility known as the "Grain Bin" is the second coronagraph station built in the Western Hemisphere. This installation, which was the first to be erected at Sacramento Peak, houses an instrument that has been particularly useful in filming a number of high quality motion pictures of the Sun's coronal motion.

Among the many ongoing research programs at Sacramento Peak Observatory is one designed to compile information about a certain type of extraordinarily intense solar eruption. A few times during each solar cycle, a highly energetic solar flare is able to penetrate to the lowest level of the Sun's atmosphere—the photosphere. When this occurs, this brilliant phenomenon can be seen in normal observations and consequently is termed a solar white-light flare (WLF). The occurrence of such a flare is rare, however; less than eighty have been recorded since Richard Carrington observed the first in 1859.

Since WLFs are extremely powerful events, in 1980 Sacramento Peak Observatory instituted a program designed to compile as much information as possible about them. The WLF observing project at Sacramento Peak is directed by D. F. Neidig, one of the world's top experts on such phenomena. The program relies on a relatively small multiband patrol instrument based on a commercially available telescope—the Questar 7.

As is true at similar installations around the globe, a number of exciting programs are in the planning and developmental stages at Sacramento Peak Observatory. Scientists are currently working to refine the Adaptive Optics System, designed to instantly correct the blurring of optical images caused by atmospheric effects. This complex instrument employs a flexible mirror controlled by dozens of small computers connected together and working as one. In addition, two newly developed instruments will monitor the magnetic fields at the Sun's surface. One measures field strengths very precisely, and the other monitors the rapid changes that occur in the magnetic structure. Such sophisticated equipment is expected to eventually provide scientists with enough information to accurately predict when and where flares will occur.

The Radiative Inputs from the Sun to the Earth (SunRISE, or RISE) project is another ongoing effort with terrestrial implications. RISE is a wide-ranging program of focused studies to characterize the variations in the Sun's radiation leading to changes in the Earth's atmosphere and environment. Such experiments help astronomers and other scientists to better understand the delicate equilibrium between the enormous energy produced by the Sun and that received at the Earth.

That balance is a focus of Wind—a spacecraft successfully launched by Delta II rocket during November 1994. The Wind spacecraft is the first of two U.S. missions of the Global Geospace Science (GGS) initiative, part of a worldwide collaboration called the International Solar-Terrestrial Physics (ISTP) program. The aim of ISTP is to understand the physical behavior of the solar-terrestrial environment in order to predict how the Earth's magnetosphere and atmosphere will respond to changes in the solar wind. The spacecraft plays a crucial role—essentially that of a scout and sentry—in the fleet of ISTP satellites. The task of Wind is to measure crucial properties of the solar wind before it impacts the Earth's magnetic field and alters the Earth's space environment and upper atmosphere in a direct manner. The other ISTP satellites will operate in special orbits and locations to measure the principal responses—sometimes dramatic disruptions from typical behavior—of the Earth's space environment to the impact of solar winds.

The second GGS satellite, Polar, will measure the flow of plasma (a solar wind of electrified particles) to and from the Earth's ionosphere. The Wind and Polar missions will perform simultaneous, and closely coordinated measurements of the key regions of Earth's nearby space environment. Data will be provided from other ISTP missions in equatorial orbits. Complementing ground-based and theoretical investigations also will be conducted.

As we move into the 21st century, solar researchers around the world are engaged in research that intuitive scientists like Galileo and pragmatists like Hale could never have envisioned. A revolution in scientific technology has occurred that will allow the Sun to be probed to previously hidden depths, measure solar magnetic fields to an accuracy never before possible, and supply extraordinarily

This photograph shows the Vacuum Tower Telescope at Sacramento Peak. The telescope collects sunlight with mirrors mounted atop a concrete pier, which rises 40 meters above the ground. The height of the pier helps to avoid ground-level atmospheric turbulence, which contributes to the motion and blurring of the image of the Sun. *Photograph courtesy of the NSO/Sacramento Peak.*

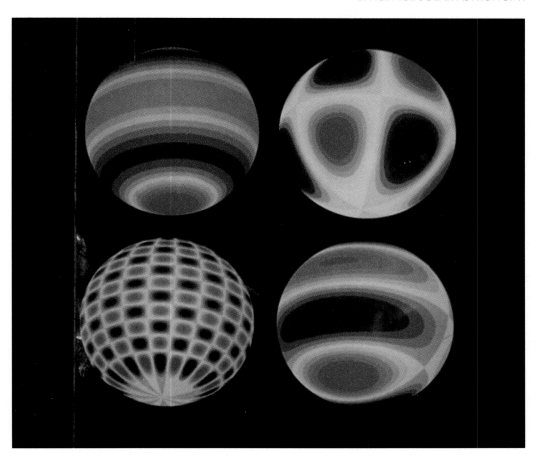

Subtle variation on the surface of the Sun with a period of 5 minutes: patterns can be seen in the gas velocity across the whole surface. These images show a few simple patterns where the blue regions represent areas of the solar surface that are rising upward, and the red regions represent areas that are sinking downward. There are actually many thousands of such patterns that rise and fall with a 5-minute period. These oscillations represent natural frequencies, and just as a ringing bell emits a sound at a certain frequency, our Sun oscillates at only certain particular frequencies. These vibrations are important since they enable astronomers to measure physical conditions inside the Sun. *Photograph courtesy of NSO/Sacramento Peak.*

detailed views of the Sun's atmosphere in all portions of the electromagnetic spectrum. The challenge of the space age has been met, but it is far from over. Meanwhile, Aristotle's "ball of pure fire" silently waits above, beckoning us into the future.

Space-Age Solar Astronomy with Your Home Computer

It has been said that today's home computer is more sophisticated than those that traveled to the Moon with the astronauts, yet many of us use ours for nothing more than record-keeping or games. New systems have now been developed that can bring the universe to your desktop. Among these public access networks are data banks with online repositories that hold a vast array of data and images of the Sun and solar activity. Much can be found on America Online and the CompuServe Information Service, but the real gems reside on the Internet.

What's available online? Probably more information than any of us could ever use! For example, the Space Environment Laboratory in Boulder, Colorado, maintains an up-to-the-minute information bank of solar activity complete with images taken just hours earlier. Want to know the status of the Wind or Geotail spacecraft missions? NASA's "Spacelink" stores fact sheets and mission status reports. Is the GONG project up and running yet? GONG newsletters and status reports are as close as your PC, as are X-ray images transmitted from the Japanese/American Yohkoh satellite.

If the space missions and ground-based projects you've read about here have piqued your curiosity and you'd like to know more, turn on the PC, subscribe to an online service, and stay informed!

The CompuServe Information Service (800-524-3388)

For current information on sunspots and solar flares and their terrestrial effects, type GO SUNSPOT. This CompuServe feature is maintained by coauthor Peter O. Taylor.

General astronomical information is available on the Astroforum (GO ASTROFORUM). Several fine images of the Sun are located in the Space Exploration Forum (GO SPACEX), and NASA has its own section (GO NASA).

America Online (800-827-6364)

The "Astronomy Club" includes up-to-date information about amateur astronomy. Several excellent images are available for download.

The Internet (Contact local providers for access information.)

The Internet is a virtually limitless group of diverse computer systems located throughout the world, available to all with a home computer equipped with a modem and the required access.

World Wide Web:

http://www.sel.noaa.gov
Space Environment Laboratory. Today's solar weather, including images and graphs.

http://info.cern.ch/Space/Overview. html
All the NASA Centers can be found in this area, plus on-line resources, computer bulletin boards, and the American Astronomical Society section.

http://www.sel.bldrdoc.gov/images/solar_sites.html
A jumping-off place for Internet sites that hold solar images from a number of

groups including Goddard Space Flight Center (Yohkoh images) and Kitt Peak Observatory.

http://sunspot.noao.edu/SP-home.html
Sacramento Peak Observatory's page, which includes visitor information and visits to the Vacuum Tower Telescope and the John W. Evans Solar Facility.

http://helios.tuc.noao.edu/gonghome.html
News of the GONG project, including a site map, images, and newsletters.

http://fits.cv.nrao.edu/www/astronomy.html
The Astro Web—a collection of pointers to astronomy-related information available on the Internet. Places of interest include the High Altitude Observatory, the National Solar Observatory at Kitt Peak, images from the Big Bear Solar Observatory (please log on before 1500 UT or after 0100 UT), and the Solar Data Analysis Center (SDAC) at NASA Goddard Space Flight Center in Greenbelt, Maryland. SDAC's resources include mission updates, solar ground and space-based images, the Yohkoh archives and eclipse bulletins. (Universal Time, or UT, is measured west from the prime meridian, which passes through Greenwich, England. There are 24 time zones around the world, each representing a change of 15 degrees, or 1 hour.)

http://www.jpl.nasa.gov
Jet Propulsion Laboratory (Pasadena, California). Latest Ulysses updates (cd public/jplinfo/news). Ulysses files are those with the prefix "UL."

The Solar Terrestrial Dispatch in cooperation with the University of Lethbridge is a supplier of time-critical solar and geophysical information. Numerous solar services are available, including major solar flare alerts, proton alerts, and daily activity summaries. Subscription requests should be directed to: oler@rho.uleth.ca

FTP Sites Worth Visiting

FTP (File Transfer Protocol) is a way of moving files from one of the computer sites on the Internet to your own computer. The FTP's we suggest visiting are called anonymous FTP'S because you log on with the username: "anonymous." (Your e-mail address is often required at the password: prompt.) These sites are open to anyone, and their files are freely available. Simply log onto the other computer, browse its files, decide what you want, and ask the remote computer to copy it to your file.

ftp sites:

ftp.sunspot.noao.edu
Corona maps, solar images (cd pub).

explorer.arc.nasa.gov
(Formerly ames.arc.nasa.gov) News and images from space missions, astronomy databases, satellites (cd pub/SPACE).

xi.uleth.ca
Aurora Images (cd pub/solar/Aurora/Images).

spacelink.msfc.nasa.gov
The NASA Bulletin Board. Information about past and future missions, including project/fact sheets, spacecraft status reports (i.e., Geotail, Wind satellites).

4

The Sun as a Star

About 4600 million years ago, the outer reaches of a huge cloud of dust and gas floating in interstellar space began to converge. We do not know for certain why it began to contract. Perhaps the contraction occurred as a result of a sudden cooling induced by pressure changes within the cloud, or it could have been stimulated by some unknown galactic pull or shock wave. When the cloud grew a bit smaller, the mutual gravitational attraction of its components took over and the inward flow of particles increased.

Eventually a dense central core formed, and as the opaque cloud rotated faster and faster, it took on a saucerlike appearance with smaller condensations of matter—destined to become planets—scattered throughout the plane of the spinning disk. (The theory that the planets condensed from a flattened nebular disk surrounding the Sun was first suggested by Pierre-Simon Laplace and Immanuel Kant in the late 18th century.)

Collisions within the inward rush of matter heated the core to ever higher temperatures until the flow was eventually matched by the outward pressure of hot gas, and the contraction abruptly halted. However, the protostar continued to radiate energy spawned by the gravitational collapse; as a result, it contracted further and its temperature continued to rise. After about ten million years, the temperature became sufficiently high, over 15 million degrees on the Kelvin temperature scale (the Kelvin scale sets its zero at absolute zero; therefore Kelvin degrees are equal to Centigrade degrees plus 273°) so that it allowed the first nuclear reactions deep in the interior to occur. A star—our Sun—was born.

During the early portion of its lifetime, the Sun was smaller and only about 70 percent as bright as today, but it was far more violent. Perhaps as a direct result of its rapid initial rotation, thought to be triple today's rate, and the consequently increased output of its magnetic dynamo, the young Sun almost certainly produced far more turbulent flares and other magnetic phenomena than it does now. Nevertheless, if we had observed the Sun in those early days we would probably not have noticed any regularities within these activities since any cyclical behavior would have been masked by powerful, random bursts of energy. Today, we can see such phenomena mirrored in the enormous flares and spectacular actions of other very young, rapidly rotating celestial objects, distant suns known as T Tauri stars.

What caused the Sun's rotational speed to drop to its present level? The answer is probably linked to the continuous flow of matter away from the Sun called the solar wind. The wind must have been much stronger when the Sun was young

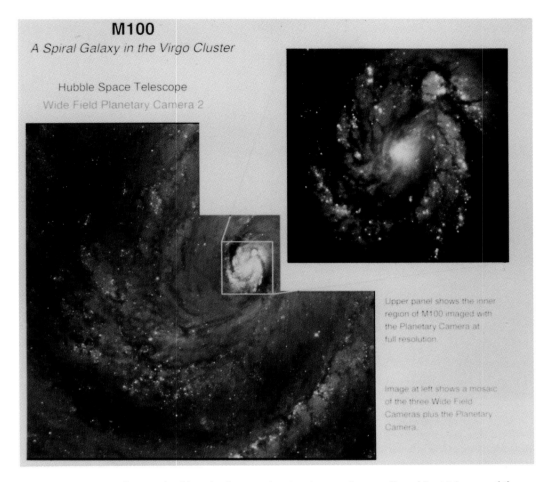

M100

A Spiral Galaxy in the Virgo Cluster

Hubble Space Telescope
Wide Field Planetary Camera 2

Upper panel shows the inner region of M100 imaged with the Planetary Camera at full resolution.

Image at left shows a mosaic of the three Wide Field Cameras plus the Planetary Camera.

The galaxy M-100 (the 100th object in the Messier Catalogue of nonstellar objects) is one of the brightest members of the Virgo Cluster of galaxies. The galaxy is in the spring constellation Coma Berenices and can be seen through a moderate-sized amateur telescope. M-100 is a spiral galaxy like our Milky Way, and is tilted face-on as seen from the Earth. If this were a photograph of the Milky Way galaxy, the solar system would be located towards the outer portion of one of the spiral's two bright arms. *Photograph courtesy of NASA.*

and very active, and the dense blast of solar particles would have carried the Sun's angular momentum (the tendency of a rotating body to continue rotating) away at a much greater rate than that detected today. In turn, its rotation would have slowed drastically, and the magnetic generation capability of the solar dynamo would have decreased to the rather sedate level we see currently.

The solar furnace

Fortunately for those of us on the Earth, after those early millennia of explosive activity ended, a state of near equilibrium has existed among the physical processes that occur within the Sun. Presently, nearly all solar radiation is a result of

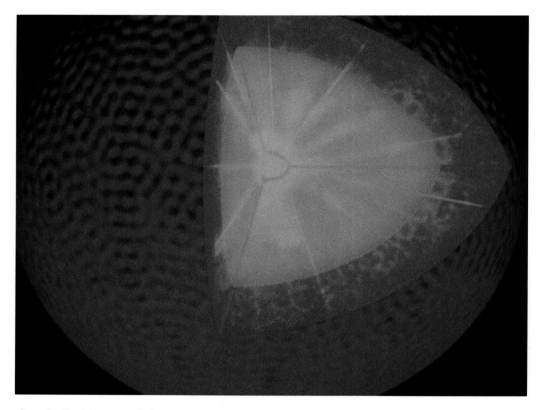

The solar interior. Knowledge of the interior of the Sun has mostly been limited to predictions from theories. However, the new study of solar global oscillations (helioseimology) has allowed some measurements of the interior to be made. Currently, theories predict that the solar core is the source of the Sun's energy; here enormous pressures and a temperature around 15 million K degrees ignite the process of nuclear fusion, in which hydrogen atoms are converted to helium. Just beyond the solar core we encounter the radiative zone, where the heat produced by nuclear reactions is carried outward by X-rays. Beyond the radiative zone is the convective zone, where gas convection transports heat and energy to the surface. *Photograph courtesy of NSO/Sacramento Peak.*

nuclear reactions in the core—a proton-proton chain during which four hydrogen protons are fused into a single helium nucleus, while radiating a tiny bit of energy. As incredible as it seems, the Sun's nuclear furnace processes an enormous amount of matter in this way: up to 700 million tons of hydrogen is converted to helium each second, and nearly 5 million tons is changed to pure energy. (For stars that are more massive than the Sun, a different nuclear process—the carbon-nitrogen-oxygen cycle—leads to a similar result.)

Astronomers are just beginning to make precision measurements of the interior structure of the Sun, however, we can draw some general theoretical conclusions from the properties and emissions observed in the past and, to some extent, from solar oscillations. We know the chemical elements that make up the Sun are the same as those on Earth, but in different proportions. In all, some 68 elements have

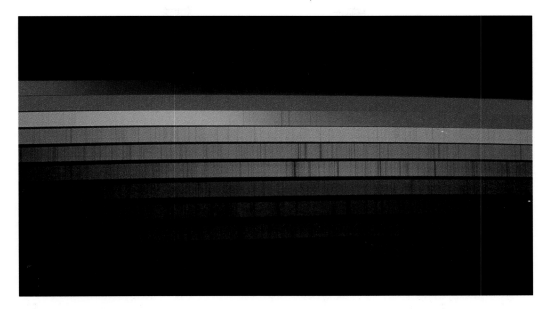

The solar spectrum in the visible, or white-light portion of the Sun's spectrum. The spectrum has been split into all its colors in this spectrogram from the National Solar Observatory. The dark bands are called absorption lines because they are created as atoms absorb light at certain wavelengths, indicating the presence of certain elements in the Sun. J. Fraunhofer discovered these spectral features in the 19th century; hence they are also known as Fraunhofer lines. *Photograph courtesy of the NOAO/National Solar Observatory.*

been identified on the Sun, with hydrogen and helium by far the most abundant.

The Sun's surface temperature is about 5800 K degrees, but the core—nearly 700,000 kilometers below the surface—reaches a temperature of over 15 million Kelvin degrees. The density at the central core is almost unimaginable, measuring about 12 times that of lead. And despite pressures at the core that are some 100,000 million times those of Earth at sea level, the core remains gaseous.

Next to the core is the radiative zone, where high-energy photons collide with electrons and ions and become light and heat. Farther out, at about 200,000 kilometers below the surface, lies the layer known as the convection zone. Here currents of gas evolve, flow upward and release energy at the surface, then flow downward to be reheated and continue the process. The circulation of these currents produces the solar granulation and gives the Sun its mottled appearance.

Still, striking as these features appear, the Sun is relatively average. Contrary to some popular beliefs, it is not a smallish, insignificant object; rather it is relatively large among neighboring suns—eighth brightest of the 100 nearest stars. If we plot the positions of a large group of stars according to their relative luminosity and temperature on a special graph—the Hertzsprung-Russell diagram—we find the Sun lies in the main sequence, near the middle of this group of youngish stars.

Luminosity, or intrinsic brightness, is mainly a factor of a star's size (i.e., surface area) and temperature, and the Sun is about average in both respects. There are

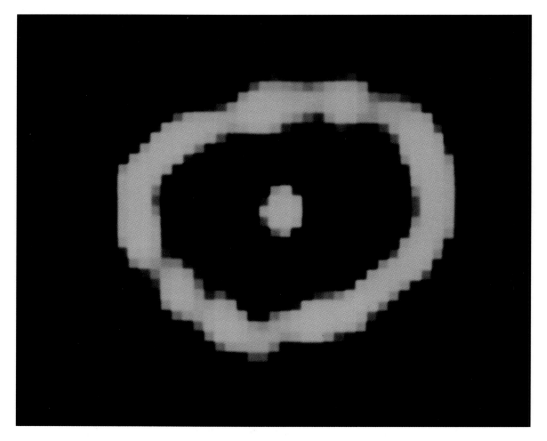

The European Space Agency's Faint Object Camera, utilizing the corrective optics provided by NASA's Corrective Optics Space Telescope Axial Replacement, has given astronomers their best look yet at a rapidly ballooning bubble of gas blasted off a star. The shell surrounds Nova Cygni 1992, which erupted on February 19, 1992. During the early part of 1994, the ring had expanded to a diameter of approximately 157 million million kilometers. *Photograph courtesy of F. Paresce and R. Jedrzejewski (STS-61) NASA/ESA.*

stars far larger in diameter, but also many that are much smaller. At the upper end of the scale we find the huge supergiants; if one of these behemoths were placed at the Sun's location it would encompass all the planets, out to and including Jupiter. The white dwarf stars lie at the opposite end of the spectrum. Many of these objects, such as the well-known companion of Sirius, are not much larger than the Earth. And of course, the bizarre neutron stars are smaller still, some perhaps only a few kilometers across, but with masses often greater than the Sun's.

Brightness is almost entirely based on surface area and temperature. If the other characteristics of two stars are approximately equal, the star with double the surface area will be about twice as bright as the other. The most luminous stars are up to a million times brighter than the Sun; placed at the Sun's location, they would immediately incinerate our planet. On the other hand, the least luminous members of the stellar community exhibit only a tiny percentage of the Sun's brilliance. If the Sun were replaced by such a star, the Earth's oceans would immediately freeze and the planet would be plunged into darkness. But again, we find that the Sun lies somewhere near the midrange of stellar brightnesses. It supplies just enough radiation to allow life to thrive here on Earth.

Finally, a star's spectrum is defined by the basic categories O, B, A, F, G, K, and M, which classify star types by temperature. The hottest stars are class O, and the coolest, class M. In the case of the Sun, we again see that at about 5800 degrees, the Sun is midrange, a class G star, accounting for its yellow-white appearance. Blue-white giants such as Spica are A-type stars with surface temperatures near 40,000 K degrees. The far cooler red giant stars such as Betelgeuse ($\approx$2500 K) are members of class M. Since temperature and luminosity are dictated mainly by mass, most stars spend a majority of their lives within the main sequence of stars outlined by the Hertzsprung-Russell diagram.

The future

The closing chapter of the Sun's existence will be written when it begins to exhaust its vast stores of hydrogen and undergoes a transformation that first takes the Sun high above its position in the main sequence, and then to the lowest levels of the Hertzsprung-Russell chart. If present calculations are correct, the Sun has expended less than half its life. During the next few thousand million years, the its rotation will slow even more and its flare and sunspot production will probably decline. Most scenarios still call for the Sun to eventually expand into an immense red giant which will grow to encompass one or more of the inner planets.

When the Sun is about 10,000 to 12,000 million years old, a combination of nuclear and other processes will have allowed the core temperature to reach an extraordinary level, perhaps upward of 300,000,000 K degrees. By then the Sun will have been burning helium for many eons and the temperature will cause a sudden brilliant eruption called a helium flash, in which a portion of the Sun will be ejected into space in a few minutes. The outpouring of emission will cause a lessening of the gravitational bonds, and at some point the Sun's outermost shells will be blown away in a huge surge of solar wind. Then for the first time the core will be exposed, surrounded by an outward-moving gas shell known as a planetary nebula.

Thereafter the Sun will spend the remainder of its stellar life as the core, a small, but extremely dense, planet-sized star known as a white dwarf. Eventually its nuclear processes will cease completely, and the Sun will pass through the rest of eternity as a cold black cinder.

Several of the Sun's physical measurements are outlined below:

Age	4.6×10^9 years
Distance from Earth	1.496×10^{13} centimeters (1 AU)
Mass	1.991×10^{33} grams
Radius	696,000 kilometers ($\approx$109 Earth radii)
Luminosity	3.85×10^{23} kilowatts
Photospheric temperature	5800 degrees Kelvin
Core temperature	15.6×10^6 degrees Kelvin

The heliopause

How large a region of space does the Sun affect? Many of us are familiar with the magnetopause, which marks the boundary between the solar wind and the Earth's magnetic field. However there is a less well known, but somewhat analogous border that encompasses the realm of the Sun; it is known as the heliopause.

The heliopause represents the frontier between the farthest reaches of the solar wind and the surrounding interstellar wind. It encloses the heliosphere, where the Sun dominates all that comes in range of its electromagnetic radiation and gravitational attraction within a huge bubble of magnetized gas. Until recently, scientists knew little about this isolated region of space where the Sun's influence merges with that of the stars.

During the last several years, however, new information about the heliopause has been obtained by sensitive instruments aboard the extraordinarily productive Voyager spacecraft. The latest data from the Voyagers suggests that the heliopause, once thought to be much closer to the center of the solar system, actually lies some 100 astronomical units (AU) distant from the Sun, about 15,000 million kilometers away. (One AU represents the average Earth-Sun distance, or about 149.6 million kilometers.) Moreover, these observations indicate that the conflict between solar and stellar winds can, at times, generate what may be the most powerful radio emission in the entire solar system, a burst that the Voyagers found to exceed 10 trillion watts of energy!

Both Voyager spacecraft, now well beyond the orbits of Neptune and Pluto, contributed to the new findings. Voyager 1 completed successful flybys of both Jupiter and Saturn and is now rising above the ecliptic plane—the great circle marked by the intersection of Earth's orbit with the celestial sphere—floating toward the stars at a distance of some 52 AU.

Voyager 2 also visited Jupiter and Saturn before completing the survey of the giant outer planets through spectacular encounters with Uranus and Neptune. The craft is currently over 40 AU from the Sun. Both vehicles were launched in 1977 and are managed by the Jet Propulsion Laboratory in Pasadena, California.

Beginning in mid-1992, the radio antennas of both spacecraft—instrument arrays known as Plasma Wave Sub-Systems—recorded mysterious low-frequency radio bursts, which are believed to emanate from the extreme edge of the solar system—the heliopause. The signals, which reached a peak several months later, were much stronger than a similar set of bursts recorded by the Voyagers in the early to mid-1980s. Such energetic explosions are not detectable on Earth, since the emission occurs at a very low frequency (2 to 3 kilohertz) that cannot penetrate the geomagnetic field. In fact, we would not even know such bursts had taken place if it were not for the Voyagers and their unique locations in space.

One interpretation of these events calls for the radio signals to be created as a cloud of electrically charged plasma expands from the Sun and interacts with the cold interstellar gas beyond the heliopause. Apparently, the intense solar activity of May and June 1991 spawned an enormous cluster of energetic particles that moved rapidly across the solar system, carried by the solar wind. Investigators believe that when the cloud of particles reached the farthest reaches of interplanetary space and slammed into the interstellar wind, a violent reaction occurred that produced the immense burst of energy recorded by the Voyagers.

A hint at the coming interaction between solar and stellar winds actually came only a few months after the solar eruptions ended, and once again the phenomenon was recorded by the ever-vigilant Voyagers. Three months after the burst of solar activity, both spacecraft recorded a sudden decline in galactic cosmic rays—the nuclei of heavy atoms born in cataclysmic events like exploding stars. Astronomers believe that these ultra-high energy particles were deflected away by a blast of solar wind hurtling through interplanetary space at a speed between 600 and 800 kilometers per second, nearly double the average wind speed.

When the Voyager measurements are compared with the solar eruptions that began this series of events, it is possible for scientists to draw some conclusions concerning the nature and location of the heliopause. They now think that boundary lies somewhere between 90 and 150 or more astronomical units from the Sun, much farther than anticipated. During the following months the emissions from the heliopause gradually changed to a higher frequency. Such changes in radio emission frequency are thought to occur as the torrent of solar wind penetrates deeper into the denser regions of the heliopause. In this case, the timing of the frequency shift indicates that the heliopause has a substantial thickness.

These discoveries, coupled with indirect measurements of the density of interplanetary plasma clouds made by arrays of ground-based radio telescopes (such as the facility operated in Gujarat, western India) supply important clues to astronomers who have long theorized about the structure of the heliosphere and the exact whereabouts of the heliopause. Equally exciting, the new findings hint at future revelations as the Voyagers continue their long journey to the farthest regions of the solar system and beyond. If the conclusions drawn from such analyses prove to be correct, the Voyager spacecraft should finally pass beyond the Sun's influence around the year 2010.

Solar irradiance

Just how much energy does the Sun radiate? Even at the Earth's distance of 150 million kilometers, the heat and light produced by the Sun are extraordinary. When the Sun is directly overhead, the energy falling on just one square meter of Earth's surface exceeds 1300 watts. At that rate nearly 2 million horsepower can be measured over a single square kilometer.

Most of us have heard the term "solar constant," not a very fitting phrase (since the value of the "constant" varies slightly) for what is more appropriately referred to as the solar irradiance. During the first half of this century a number of systematic measurements of this quality were made from ground-based observatories, chief among them the long series of observations under the direction of C. G. Abbot of the Smithsonian Institution.

The first measurements of solar irradiation, however, were obtained in 1837 by the Frenchman C. S. M. Pouillet, using a device consisting of a blackened container filled with water. A thermometer inserted into the liquid recorded changes in the rate of temperature increase when the instrument was moved from the

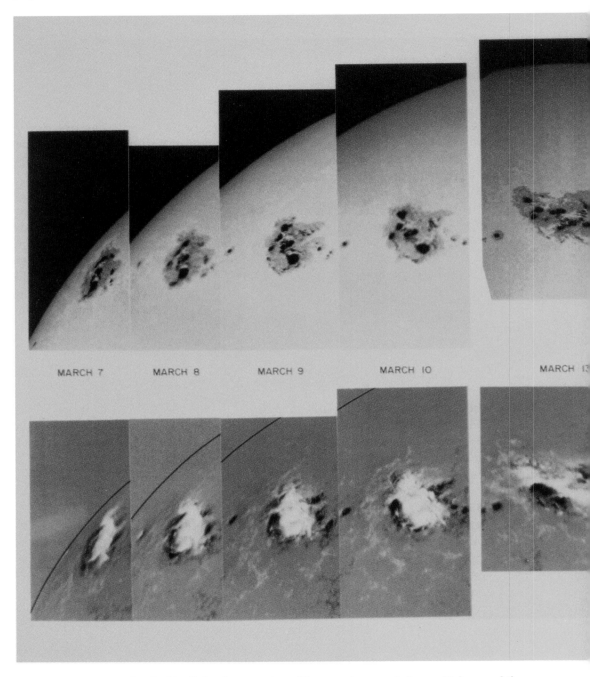

MARCH 7   MARCH 8   MARCH 9   MARCH 10   MARCH 13

A mosaic of white-light photographs, with magnetograms below, which record the March 1989 disk transit of NOAA/USAF Region 5395. Region 5395 produced many powerful flares, gamma ray, and emission events. The dip in the Sun's irradiance during the group's passage across the visible hemisphere is shown in the accompanying diagram. *Photograph courtesy of NOAO/Kitt Peak.*

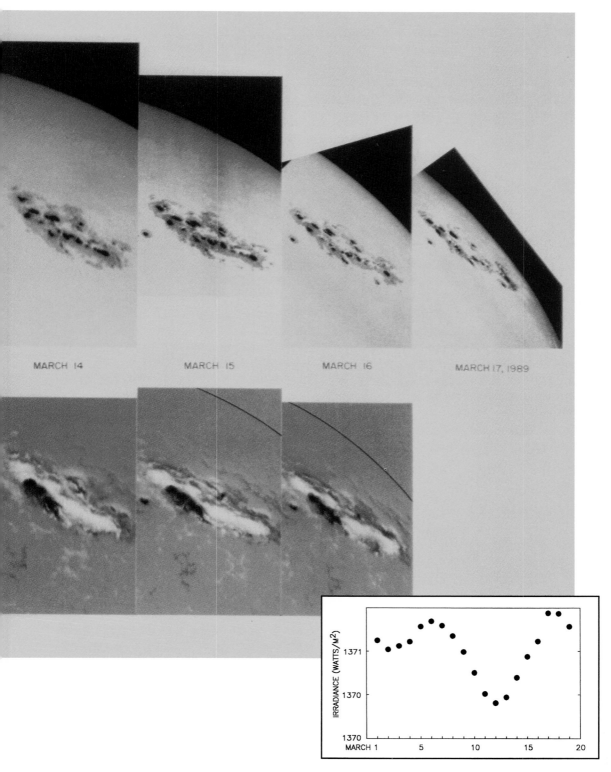

MARCH 14 · MARCH 15 · MARCH 16 · MARCH 17, 1989

shade to sunlight. Pouillet determined a value of 1260 watts per square meter (W/m^2) with his experiment, an excellent result in view of modern observations, which show a value near 1368 W/m^2.

Instruments such as Pouillet's are called pyrheliometers. They were eventually replaced by electronic devices that compare the heat generated by the Sun with that of a fixed electrical current. The Smithsonian program, begun by S. P. Langley in 1902 and directed by Abbot until 1960, used similar instruments—in this instance, the bolometer developed by Langley and calibrated by a special silver-disk pyrheliometer built by Abbot. A recent reanalysis of the Smithsonian measurements resulted in a mean value of 1353 W/m^2 for the irradiation component.

The data obtained by Abbot indicated that the irradiance was approximately constant, at least within an uncertainty of about 1 percent. Unfortunately, even though these data were acquired at mountain-top sites they still suffered from atmospheric absorption—mainly by ozone and water vapor—so the measurements need large corrections to make the data useful. Such problems have now been largely overcome through the use of spacecraft and balloon-borne experiments, which place monitors high above the densest portion of the Earth's atmosphere.

When solar energy reaches Earth it heats the atmosphere, surface, and oceans. Most infrared radiation is absorbed by carbon dioxide and water vapor as it travels through the atmosphere, and a portion escapes into space. Without this atmospheric absorption, Earth's temperature could not support most forms of life.

There are, however, large differences in the average amount of solar energy received at any one location of the Earth's surface (the solar insolation). Moreover, the amount is often far less (some 20 percent on the average) than the total solar irradiance. The more pronounced of such variations occur because of latitude differences and time effects. For example, the annual amount of solar energy received in the Earth's equatorial regions is over twice as great as at the poles, where the Sun is below the horizon for a portion of the year.

Time effects are mainly related to seasonal changes. During the summer any terrestrial location receives more energy because the Sun is higher in the sky and daylight is longer. The result is somewhat complicated by other conditions, such as the dissimilarity in energy storage capability between land and sea (water has the greater capacity). But this factor more than compensates for additional radiation received during January, when the Earth is closer to the Sun than it is in July.

Recent measurements of the solar irradiance are obtained with devices such as active cavity radiometers (ACRs), which typically consist of two identical blackened, cone-shaped cavities and an electronic servo system. The electrical system is usually designed to keep one of the cavities—the primary—at a slightly higher temperature than the secondary, or "reference" cavity. Sunlight enters the primary cavity through a shutter, causing it to heat up. The differing power requirements between open and closed conditions provide a good estimate of solar irradiance.

Today the best data are obtained with spacecraft ACRs—in effect, electrically self-calibrated pyrheliometers that are uniformly sensitive from the extreme ultraviolet to the far infrared. One group of irradiance instrumentation was placed into Earth orbit during October 1984 aboard NASA's Earth Radiation Budget Satellite

(ERBS). According to the National Geophysical Data Center in Boulder, Colorado, data is collected and processed by the ERBS system in the following way:

Total solar irradiance measures the sunlight falling each second on one square meter of surface above our atmosphere. Individual solar irradiance values represent instantaneous measurements, which are normalized to the mean Earth-Sun distance. Once every two weeks the monitor observes the Sun for several 64-second intervals, each separated into half periods. During the first such period the Sun drifts across the field of view, and its radiation is measured.

During the second period a low-emittance shutter, representative of a near-zero irradiation source, is cycled into the field of view and its radiation field is measured. The resulting measurements from the two periods are compared to define the Sun's irradiance. Measurement precision is approximately 0.01 percent with an accuracy near 0.02 percent. Similar monitoring systems have operated on the Upper Atmosphere Research Satellite, the NOAA 9 and NOAA 10 space platforms, on ERBS, and on Solar Maximum Mission, Nimbus 7, and other spacecraft.

Solar activity levels

Now, returning to the question implied by our original statement, just how constant is the solar irradiation? The answer is, not very! In one instance, over the short term, the transit of a large sunspot group across the Sun's disk produced a conspicuous decline in radiation emitted from the photosphere. Conversely, when sunspot activity is low and few if any spot groups are present on the visible hemisphere, irradiation rises to comparatively high levels. As a result, when intensity-corrected, total sunspot areas are compiled over time, it is possible to determine an irradiance deficit that is directly attributable to sunspot presence.

Where is that missing radiation, and how does the passage of a large sunspot group produce this effect? Since it is highly unlikely that energy generation deep within the Sun is precisely mimicked by photospheric activity (it takes radiation well over a million years to rise from the solar core to the Sun's surface, and any variations would be smoothed together in the process), the energy blocked by the relatively cooler spot group must reappear in some form at a future time.

Some explanations of this effect suggest that the energy is stored within the group's magnetic field and reradiated later, while others propose that it is otherwise redirected, perhaps into magnetic wave motion. A few investigators also suspect that faculae—the large, bright-looking areas frequently associated with sunspots—play a prominent role in this process.

According to the National Geophysical Data Center, when measured over relatively long intervals, irradiance measurements depict a star that dims slightly during sunspot minimum and brightens around maximum, reaching a peak a little after the maximum sunspot number. Observed brightness changes are small, but surveys suggest that the Sun's luminosity varies by several percent over the solar cycle. For those of us with a mathematical interest, the irradiance (I) can be related to sunspot number and the Sun's 10.7 centimeter radio flux as follows:

I = 1366.82 + 7.71 x 10^{-3} sunspot number, and, I = 1366.27 + 8.98 x 10^{-3} radio flux.

But wait, the irradiance also shows an additional long-term change. In view of this second variation, is the Sun then a variable star with multiple periods? And what, if any, physical changes to the Sun accompany—or perhaps usher in—such apparently anomalous solar behavior? Recent information seems to show that the solar luminosity, and therefore its irradiance, may in fact fluctuate regularly, accompanied by both changes in the Sun's size and effective surface temperature.

Sabatino Sofia and his colleagues at NASA and Yale have discovered evidence to indicate that a prolonged interval of low activity is associated with a low level of irradiance and an increased solar radius. This investigation has shown that the Sun's size appears to vary over a period of about 90 years, and that its radius was nearly 0.5 second of arc larger than average at the beginning and end of the 19th century. A similar period, related to regular amplitude variations within the series of historical sunspot cycles—the Gleissberg cycle—has long been suspected.

In the past, measurements that mark the transit of Mercury or the moon's passage across the solar disk during an eclipse have been used to monitor the Sun's diameter. Changes on the order of 400 kilometers (0.6 second of arc) to a "normal" solar radius of a bit less than 700,000 kilometers are well documented. Unfortunately, until the advent of the space age technology discussed above, precise measurements of solar irradiance were much more difficult to obtain.

Ironically, irradiance can now be measured with greater accuracy than the Sun's diameter. In the near future, more accurate information gathered by instruments like the NASA/USAF Solar Disk Sextant will allow precise measurements. For the moment, however, multiple solar pulsation continues to intrigue.

Planetary systems

For many years the Sun was the only star known to have a family of planets. As we might expect, this has been a subject of debate, with nearly all astronomers believing that many, if not a majority, of stars are orbited by satellite worlds. Recent observations seem to confirm these conclusions. Moreover, several studies made with the Hubble Space Telescope indicate planetary systems may be common.

This research suggests that when a star forms from an interstellar cloud of dust and gas, it is frequently accompanied by a massive disk from which planets later condense, as was the case with our own Sun and solar system. Interestingly, these studies indicate that the rate of occurrence for such systems seems to be approximately 50 percent, so once again the Sun may fall into the range of average stars.

Many stars have been discovered that vary in brightness and produce sunspots ("starspots"), flares, and other active phenomena. The common denominator linking them with the Sun may be the role played by magnetic fields. Only through a detailed knowledge of similar effects on the Sun can these events be understood.

Like a steady and dependable spouse, the Sun is rarely fully appreciated. Nonetheless, we have, right here in our own backyard, a fine example of a typical star, one that can be readily investigated by both amateur and professional astronomers using a variety of simple and complex equipment, not the least of which is spacecraft Earth itself.

The Sun as a Star

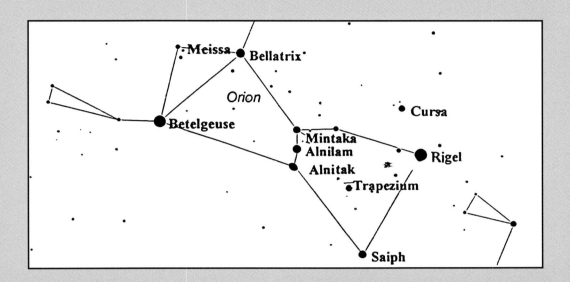

In Chapter 4 we learned that stars are classified according to their spectral type, with type O stars the hottest and type M the coolest. Stars of each type display a characteristic tinge of color corresponding to their surface temperature (see chart on page 66). Can you detect these differences visually? Fortunately, with the aid of binoculars or a telescope with good optical qualities we can actually see color variations between many of the brighter stars.

For example, even to the unaided eye, the type M star Antares, in the constellation Scorpius, has such a distinctly red appearance that novices often confuse it with Mars, the so-called "Red Planet." And with even a pair of small 7 x 35 mm binoculars, the class B giant, Rigel, sparkles like a blue diamond. Try to see these differences yourself with the aid of the simple star charts we have included and a telescope or binoculars. Then see if you can detect the yellow hue generated by Capella. (Portions of these star charts were generated by "The Sky," a computer program available through Software Bisque.)

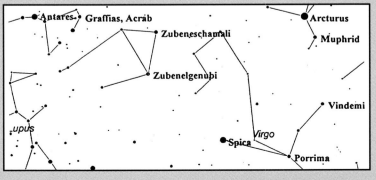

65

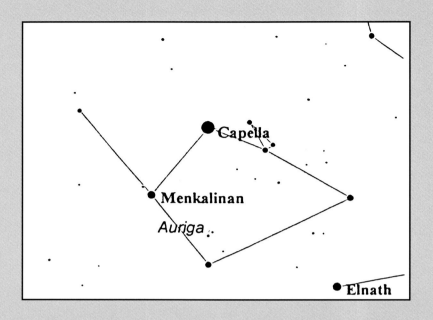

Class	Average Temperature (K°)	Characteristics
O	40,000	violet, short-lived, lines of ionized helium
Examples: Zeta Ophiuchi, Iota Orionis		
B	20,000	blue, lines of neutral helium
Examples: Rigel, Spica		
A	10,000	blue, hydrogen lines, weak ionized calcium
Examples: Sirius, Vega		
F	7,500	blue-white, weak ionized calcium
Examples: Canopus, Polaris		
G	5,500	white-yellow, medium ionized calcium, many metals
Examples: the Sun, Capella		
K	4,500	orange-red, strong ionized calcium
Examples: Aldebaran, Arcturus		
M	3,000	red, strong bands of titanium oxide
Examples: Antares, Betelgeuse		

The spectral types are further divided into subcategories, for example, K0, K1, K2 . . . K9, followed by M0, and so forth. Astronomers measure star colors with electronic photometers equipped with a specific set of special filters.

5

Features Above and Beneath the Photosphere

The lowest level of the Sun's atmosphere—the tenuous surface of the Sun visible in white light—is called the photosphere ("light-sphere"). Line-of-sight measurements of the photospheric emission at the center of the solar disk give a temperature of almost 6400 K degrees. However, if we shift our attention away from the depths of the photosphere to the limb, or edge of the Sun's disk, where only its uppermost layer can be measured, the temperature drops by nearly 2000 K degrees, and we arrive at an average photospheric temperature of ≈5800 K degrees. Since the temperature decreases as we move away from the lower photospheric levels, we would expect the limb emission to be redder, and it is. These effects combine to cause the well-known phenomenon of "limb-darkening," a feature familiar to all who observe and photograph the Sun.

Solar granulation

In our mind's eye, we may think of the photosphere as a smooth gaseous shell, but this is not the case. Instead, the entire solar surface is made up of a myriad of comparatively small "granules," convective cells of gas rising from within the Sun. Groups of these cells glimpsed through small telescopes produce a mottled or "orange-peel" appearance.

Although the granules vary in size, they frequently assume the shape of irregular polygons about 1100 kilometers across. They are surrounded by a dark intergranular network which reflects cooler gases that have sunk to a slightly lower level. During their growth stage the granules become several hundred degrees hotter than the intergranular lanes as they expand upward with a mean velocity

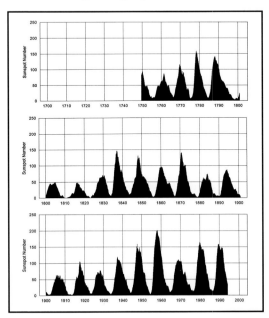

Figure 5.1. Smoothed monthly sunspot numbers, circa 1755–1994. *Diagram courtesy of the National Geophysical Data Center.*

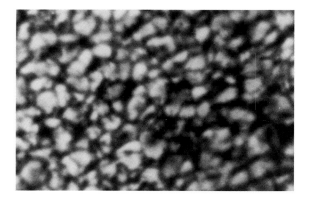

A high-resolution photograph of the solar granulation. Note the erupting granules near the center of this picture. *Photograph courtesy of Sacramento Peak Observatory.*

of about 2 kilometers per second. If our hearing were properly sensitive and sound could travel through the near vacuum of interplanetary space, we could hear a powerful low roar caused by sound waves emanating from the vast granular system, drowning out a pronounced solar oscillation with a period of about 5 minutes (the Sun is known to oscillate in nearly 10 million different modes). This continuously changing network of convective cells leads a chaotic existence of growth, fragmentation, decay, and explosion.

The first really good photographs of the solar granulation were obtained by Pierre Janssen in the 19th century. Janssen's photos were so good, in fact, that they were not bettered until the Stratoscope balloon-borne experiment carried out by M. Schwarzschild shortly after World War II. Recently, the resolution of granular images has been improved even further. Some superb ground-based photographs have been obtained at the Pic du Midi Observatory under excellent seeing conditions, but the most exciting views have probably been garnered by spacecraft, which avoid the effects of Earth's unstable atmosphere. One such project, the granular "movies" taken by the Solar Optical Universal Polarimeter (SOUP) on Spacelab 2, has achieved a resolution of about 0.25 arc second, which means that a solar feature as small as 175 kilometers across can be observed.

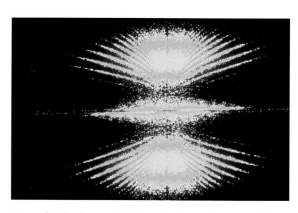

A graph of solar oscillations by the astronomer John Harvey. The frequency (vertical axis) and the number per unit distance (horizontal axis) of oscillations of the surface of the Sun are shown. Very low frequency and large spatial scale are at the center of the diagram. The ridges show that the structure of the Sun produces cavities for sound waves much like an organ pipe. *Photograph courtesy of NOAO/ National Solar Observatory.*

The ultra-high resolution SOUP movies illustrate that exploding granules—cells that expand rapidly and frequently develop a dark central core—are a routine feature of granular evolution, although they were once thought to occur only rarely. When such cells erupt they have a profound effect on neighboring granules, which are pushed away and destroyed or distorted by the exploder. Even though the lifetime of an average granule is short—about 18 minutes, including growth and decay phases—the life of an individual granule varies greatly since it is dramatically influenced by events in its immediate location. It is interesting to note that while a high percentage (about 40 percent) of granules are exploders, they almost never appear in the strongly magnetized areas around sunspots.

Exploding granules seem to repeat and may produce new exploders, but they are not evenly distributed over the Sun's surface. There appears to be no regular pattern of granular evolution. Instead, the solar surface is comprised of brightness fluctuations caused by a combination of convection, turbulence, sound waves and magnetic fields. There is still much to be learned about the solar granulation, but this new knowledge has considerably changed the long-standing concept of a "quiet" Sun and will almost certainly alter our understanding of the properties of the Sun's convection system.

Is there a pattern to the movements of solar granules? Several years ago solar scientists at the Pic du Midi Observatory learned that great clumps of granules move together within mesogranules, large groups of cells 5,000 to 10,000 kilometers across. The movement and boundaries of such formations can be traced by measuring the distribution of numerous tiny network bright points, small features that appear where packets of magnetic field lines break the Sun's surface.

These studies have shown that the mesogranules themselves are pulled around by even larger structures up to 30,000 kilometers wide, located just beneath the Sun's surface. These are the supergranules, which should not be confused with even larger convection waves discussed later on.

Apparently mesogranules near the center of a supergranule meander about randomly, but those located farther away tend to migrate toward its edge and dissolve. While the general outline of mesogranules can be determined through bright points and the movements of granules, the supergranulation cannot be seen in normal observations. Rather, supergranules, which last about a day, are detected through their velocity flow patterns expressed by a small displacement of their spectral lines. All these features—granules, mesogranules and supergranules—are convective circulations driven by heat welling up from the solar interior. As you might expect, the flows associated with these phenomena interact with magnetic fields rising from deep within the Sun to cause a wide variety of effects at the surface.

Sunspot cycles

Sunspots are the most obvious of these features and have been noted throughout most of human history. All sunspot groups begin their lives as relatively tiny cells called pores, which form as the first bits of magnetic flux, carried upward by rising gas cells, complete their journey and invade the photosphere. Many pores are short-lived and last for only an hour or so, but others form the basis of huge sunspot groups which are many times larger than the Earth and can last for several months. A new spot group first appears when pores coalesce and form the dark, or umbral, portion of a sunspot. Often these are tiny spots without a penumbra, the filamented structure that frequently surrounds the central umbra of a mature spot. Most groups have an optically bipolar configuration; that is, they are composed of two principal spots oriented in a general west-to-east direction. These prominent features are referred to as the group's leading (or preceding) and trailing (or following) spots.

The new spot group grows larger as more magnetic flux penetrates the area where the first tiny spot formed, sometimes to a point where it encompasses over 100 individual umbrae. Areas of newly erupting flux are referred to as emerging flux regions or simply EFRs. Sunspot lifetimes vary from hours to months, during which the outer reaches of the new group wage a constant war with the seething photosphere surrounding it. At some point the emerging flux diminishes and the cluster begins to lose the battle. Thereafter, the group decays in a rough reversal of its growth pattern and eventually disappears altogether.

Why do sunspot umbrae appear so dark? The exact mechanism is not fully understood, but it is almost certainly related to the strong magnetic fields inherent in all spot groups. Magnetic fields inhibit the flow of turbulent convective motions, and consequently a spot region develops a lower temperature than the surrounding photosphere. The difference is fairly substantial—in the neighborhood of 2000 K degrees—which results in an average sunspot temperature of about 3800 K degrees. Still, the spots are not exactly frigid, even though they seem dark when compared with the brilliant photosphere—if viewed by themselves they would appear brighter than the Full Moon.

In 1770 University of Glasgow professor A. O. Wilson won the astronomical award given by the Science Society of the University of Copenhagen for his suggestion that sunspots formed shallow depressions in the photosphere. Wilson's observations of large circular spots near the Sun's limb seemed to show that the umbra was displaced toward the center of the solar disk as the spot neared the limb (an effect Wilson believed was caused by openings in a glowing outer solar shell). However, we are not so sure today, since the effect seems to be missing in many observations. It is possible that the higher transparency of the colder, and therefore thinner, spot material contributes to the Wilson effect.

A different kind of growth and decay—the rise and fall in the numbers of sunspots that we call the sunspot cycle—is one of the most fascinating of the Sun's properties. The relative sunspot number that defines each cycle (see Chapters 2 and 10) is the longest continuous record of astronomical activity. The study of this record and the forecasting of current activity and future sunspot cycles is all the more intriguing because such cycles provide a good indication of the rate of activity for many of the Sun's other active phenomena. Beginning in 1755, each cycle is numbered consecutively according to a scheme devised in the 1930s at the Swiss Federal Observatory in Zurich, Switzerland.

The maximum sunspot number varies considerably from cycle to cycle, so it is possible to group past cycles into categories according to their maximum intensity and use the information to classify and predict the activity level for a current cycle. The record can be divided into three general classes based on a running average, or "smoothed," (monthly) relative sunspot number: weak cycles with a peak intensity less than 90; moderate cycles with peaks between 90 and 140; and strong cycles with maximum intensities that exceed 140. Only five recorded cycles have reached a maximum amplitude of 150 or more (four of these have occurred recently), and just one has exceeded 200. The parameters for cycles 1 through 22 (1755–1994) are summarized in Table 5.1.

Most cycles share several characteristics. Their durations are similar (although recent cycles have been both shorter and of greater amplitude than the average cycle), and their rise rates seem to be tied to their maximum amplitudes. Since a majority of cycles do have about the same 11-year length, the stronger cycles exhibit steep ascents to a relatively high maximum, followed by a slow decline. At the other end of the spectrum, weak cycles are much more symmetrical. There is also a strong tendency for cycles to alternate between higher and lower maxima, depending on whether a cycle is odd-numbered or even-numbered, respectively.

Sunspot prediction

The correlation between rise rate and maximum intensity provides a means of predicting the maximum of the next cycle. Comparing the rising branch of a new cycle with a series of mean curves derived from previous sunspot cycles provides some indication of the strength and timing of the next maximum. The onetime director of the Swiss Federal Observatory, Max Waldmeier, found that the curves of all cycles, regardless of their intensity, intersect around a common point—near a monthly mean value of 50. According to Waldmeier, the following maximum will then occur about 21 months later. This method produces reasonably good results, except for a small number of high-amplitude cycles. Statistical techniques such as the McNish-Lincoln method also attempt to relate current activity with past performance, but tend to regress toward the average and share the drawback of few previous high-maxima cycles.

Richard Thompson of the Australian IPS Radio and Space Services has recently developed one of the more promising prediction methods. Thompson's technique is one of the relatively new "precursor" methods, which are based on correlations between a new cycle's amplitude and phenomena observed or originating on the Sun during the declining phase of a current cycle. Precursor methods frequently make use of the extensive record of geomagnetic disturbance indices such as the occurrence and effects of coronal holes (Chapter 6).

The Thompson procedure is based on the amount of strong recurrent geomagnetic storm disturbances that develop during a cycle's decline as a result of coronal hole activity. This method has proven to be very accurate when applied to both current and past activity cycles. Moreover, it is simple to apply and gives a very early indication of the impending cycle's maximum intensity. However, other techniques must be used to predict the timing of the new maximum.

Unfortunately, the sunspot cycle does not lend itself easily to prediction. All current forecasting techniques are prone to uncertain results that may be compounded by the presence of hidden periodicities in the Sun's activity. During the past 150 years a number of astronomers have suggested secondary and even tertiary periods, although the evidence appears to be strongest for a secondary cycle

			TABLE 5.1				
Cycle	Begin	Maximum	End	SSN	Length	Rise	Fall
1	1755 Mar	1761 Jun	1766 May	86.5	11.25 yr	6.25 yr	5.00 yr
2	1766 Jun	1769 Sep	1775 May	115.8	9.00	3.25	5.75
3	1775 Jun	1778 May	1784 Aug	158.5	9.25	2.92	6.33
4	1784 Sep	1788 Feb	1798 Apr	141.2	13.67	3.42	10.25
5	1798 May	1805 Feb	1810 Jul	49.2	12.25	6.75	5.50
6	1810 Aug	1816 Apr	1823 Apr	48.7	12.75	5.67	7.08
7	1823 May	1829 Nov	1833 Oct	71.7	10.50	6.50	4.00
8	1833 Nov	1837 Mar	1843 Jun	146.9	9.67	3.33	6.33
9	1843 Jul	1848 Feb	1855 Nov	131.6	12.42	4.58	7.83
10	1855 Dec	1860 Feb	1867 Feb	97.9	11.25	4.17	7.08
11	1867 Mar	1870 Aug	1878 Nov	140.5	11.75	3.42	8.33
12	1878 Dec	1883 Dec	1890 Feb	74.6	11.25	5.00	6.25
13	1890 Mar	1894 Jan	1901 Dec	87.9	11.83	3.83	8.00
14	1902 Jan	1906 Feb	1913 Jul	64.2	11.58	4.08	7.50
15	1913 Aug	1917 Aug	1923 Jul	105.4	10.00	4.00	6.00
16	1923 Aug	1928 Apr	1933 Aug	78.1	10.08	4.67	5.42
17	1933 Sep	1937 Apr	1944 Jan	119.2	10.42	3.58	6.83
18	1944 Feb	1947 May	1954 Mar	151.8	10.17	3.25	6.92
19	1954 Apr	1958 Mar	1964 Sep	201.3	10.50	3.92	6.58
20	1964 Oct	1968 Nov	1976 May	110.6	11.67	4.08	7.58
21	1976 Jun	1979 Dec	1986 Aug	164.5	10.25	3.50	6.75
22	1986 Sep	1989 Jul	— —	158.1	—	2.83	—
Average:				113.8	11.02	4.20	6.73

of about 80 to 90 years in length. Such a cycle was originally proposed by Rudolf Wolf, but has come to be known as the "Gleissberg Cycle" after its main proponent, German astronomer Wolfgang Gleissberg.

Several of these scenarios adequately reproduce past activity, but none has been infallible in making predictions. The comparatively short period of reliable sunspot determinations makes the detection of long-term cycles very difficult, and such cycles may have a significant impact on the 11-year cycle. Consequently, the sunspot cycle and the 22-year magnetic cycle (see below) are the only periods for which the evidence is indisputable.

In addition to measurements of sunspot activity, a cycle can also be monitored by recording the fluctuation of the Sun's radio output, often at a frequency of 2800 megahertz (10.7 centimeters), but also at other wavelengths. Solar radio flux emissions originate in the higher regions of the chromosphere and lower corona, and generally parallel the sunspot index. Daily variations (adjusted to a standard Earth-Sun distance of one astronomical unit) have only been determined since 1947, so this record cannot be used for long-term studies of solar variability.

Irregularities in the cycle

Substantial irregularities in the sunspot cycle have occurred, although it appears that they are rare. The prolonged lull in sunspot emergence called the "Maunder

Minimum," which took place between 1645 and 1715, and the more poorly defined Spörer Minimum (1450 to 1550?) point up this puzzling aspect of the cycle.

For a time, the reality of such strange lapses in sunspot activity was in question. However, an extensive analysis by John Eddy in the 1970s put most doubts to rest, at least for the Maunder Minimum. Eddy searched the historical records and unearthed a number of comments by well-known astronomers pointing to the absence of spots; he listed

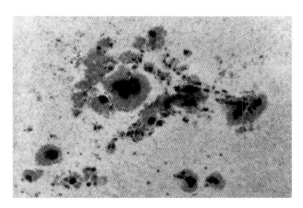

This giant array of sunspots appeared on the Sun near the end of October 1991. *Photograph courtesy of French astronomer J. Dragesco.*

corroborative evidence in the form of observations of aurorae (very few) and the amount of the radioactive isotope ^{14}C found in tree rings. Radioactive carbon is created by the collision of galactic cosmic rays (the nuclei of atoms traveling at near the speed of light, which are thought to be produced in stellar explosions) and nitrogen atoms in the Earth's atmosphere; it is measurable because a portion of the carbon enters the life chain of plants and animals. When solar activity is high, magnetic fields carried out from the Sun in the solar wind shield the Earth from such radiation, and less ^{14}C is produced. However, Eddy found a significant increase in ^{14}C during the period of missing sunspots, indicating that the Sun was uncharacteristically quiet in this interval.

Astronomers are not certain of a mechanism that could cause such a disruption. They have suggested a number of explanations, ranging from an interaction among long-term cycles to complex scenarios that deal with the physics of the solar dynamo itself. Astronomer John Eddy best summarized the debate when he concluded, "the reality of the Maunder Minimum and its implications of basic solar change may be but one more defeat in our long and losing battle to keep the sun perfect, or if not perfect, constant, and if inconstant, regular. . . ."

Emergence and movement of sunspot groups

Shortly after the first telescopic observations of sunspots, it was realized that sunspots are not evenly distributed over the Sun's surface but are concentrated in 35-degree-wide belts on each side of the solar equator. An important property of each solar cycle concerns the way that groups of spots emerge within these circumsolar bands.

In the 1850s, the English astronomer Richard Carrington discovered that the onset of each sunspot cycle coincides with a sudden appearance of new spots at notably higher latitudes than those that erupt near the end of the cycle. At the beginning of the 20th century, a second English astronomer, Edward W. Maunder (for whom the Maunder Minimum is named), and his wife, Annie S. D.

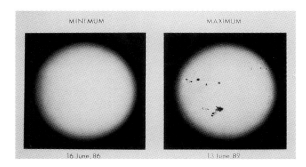

Slow changes occur on the Sun, a gradual cyclic variation called the solar cycle. The solar cycle is a many-year cycle in which the number of sunspots visible on the Sun varies. In this image we see the full disk of the Sun at two instants in a solar cycle: one image near the minimum, and one image near the maximum of cycle number 22. The sunspot number oscillates from 0 to around 200 and then back to 0 in the course of an average 11-year cycle. *Photograph courtesy of the National Solar Observatory/Sacramento Peak.*

Maunder, studied this phenomenon. While the Maunders were engaged in this research, they developed a graph known as the butterfly diagram (so-called because of its distinctive shape, which resembles the outstretched wings of a butterfly) that plots the latitudes of emerging groups of spots against time. Such graphs clearly confirm Carrington's discovery.

Sometime after the publication of the Maunders' research, astronomers became aware of an overlap in the sunspot cycle. That is, for a year or two after the first spots of a new cycle appear, groups representing both the old and new cycle exist together. Typically, the first spots from a new cycle emerge 12 to 18 months before the end of the current cycle, at a solar latitude of around 25 degrees.

When the old cycle comes to an official end (that is, at the time of minimum in the smoothed monthly sunspot index—the intersection of the falling and rising cycles), spots from the new cycle emerge at slightly higher latitudes, and the next cycle is underway. After the spots reach a peak and the cycle begins to decline, groups of spots appear at increasingly lower latitudes until the cycle ends with groups that erupt near the equator at an average latitude of about 7 degrees.

A cycle may also evolve unequally in each solar hemisphere. For example, during cycle 22 the number of spots in the Northern Hemisphere reached a maximum in mid-1989, but the peak in the Southern Hemisphere was delayed for another two years. A cycle's maximum amplitude can also be greater in one hemisphere than in the other. The Southern Hemisphere dominated during cycle 18, and again during cycle 22, but for cycles 19 through 21 sunspot activity was strongest in the north. It is also common for a cycle to alternate activity between hemispheres as it develops. (The Northern Hemisphere dominated until just after the maximum of cycle 22, was then exceeded by activity in the Southern Hemisphere until late in the cycle when activity was mixed.) Those factors seem to vary at random and do not appear to follow any set rule.

What causes this strange pattern of sunspot emergence? Although it may originate as rising magnetic fields are wound together and stretched by the Sun's differential rotation, as suggested by H. W. Babcock and his colleagues in the 1960s, others attribute the process to torsional oscillation. According to this concept, initially the work at Mt. Wilson Observatory in 1980 of Robert Howard and Barry Labonte, zones of faster rotation originate at the poles and drift to the equator in

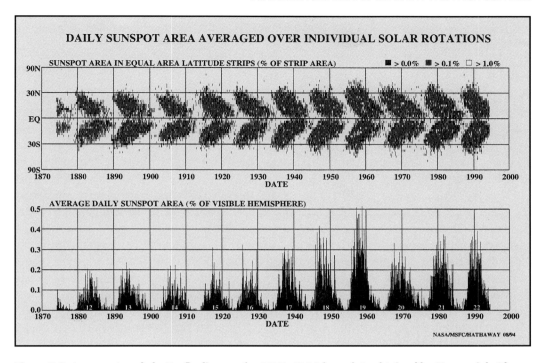

Figure 5.2. A sunspot cycle butterfly diagram for 1874–1994 from data obtained by Greenwich Observatory and the NOAA/USAF SOON network. The bottom panel shows how much of the visible surface of the Sun was covered by sunspots for each rotation of the Sun since 1874. The upper panel shows how much of each of 50 equal-area latitude strips from the South Pole to the North was covered by sunspots. In color, black would indicate the presence of small spots; red, between 0.1 and 1.0 percent of the strip was covered; and yellow, that more than 1.0 percent of the strip was occupied by sunspots during that rotation of the Sun. This shows how sunspots first appear in two latitude bands at about 30 degrees north and south at the beginning of a cycle, and how these bands grow and move toward the equator as the cycle progresses. *Diagram courtesy of D. Hathaway, NASA/MSFC.*

about 22 years. This scenario calls for new-cycle sunspots to emerge soon after the maximum rate reaches a latitude of 30 degrees North or South.

In 1987 a mechanism was proposed that could provide a key to this research. H. Snodgrass and P. Wilson suggested that huge waves of convection exist beneath the solar supergranulation, which enhance rising magnetic fields by continually forcing them into the Sun's interior where they compress and strengthen. The waves are believed to originate near the Sun's poles and gradually move the magnetic concentrations through a network of currents toward the equator. Presumably, when the material reaches the normal spot latitudes years later, the magnetic fields are so intensified they are able to break the solar surface and form sunspots.

Such theories indicate that the solar cycle does not really begin with the emergence of spots high in the sunspot zone, but is triggered by the onset of a much higher-latitude wave during the descending branch of an old cycle. These concepts would be incompatible with most of the traditional solar activity models and would support a growing body of evidence showing that the phenomenon first unearthed by Carrington is but one manifestation of a complex process in which sunspots play only a minor role.

Sunspot polarity

In addition to their optical appearance, many sunspot groups are also magnetically bipolar—that is, they contain opposite magnetic polarities in leading and trailing spots. And with few exceptions, the dominant magnetic polarity of the leading spot for spot groups in the Sun's Northern Hemisphere is the reverse of those in the south.

The preceding (more westerly) spots of Northern Hemisphere groups normally possess positive polarity during odd-numbered cycles, while southern leaders are negative. (In any cycle, roughly 2 to 3 percent of the groups show a "reversed" or irregular, magnetic polarity. Occasionally a complex group with irregular polarity will demonstrate a high level of activity, but studies show that in general, these groups are no more or less active than groups with normal polarity.) The overall hemispherical polarity reverses at about the time that an old sunspot cycle ends (the Hale-Nicholson law). Thus each hemisphere returns to its original polarity at 22-year intervals (i.e., every two sunspot cycles), forming the solar magnetic cycle.

The leading spot of a bipolar group is usually located closer to the solar equator than the trailing spot, a characteristic known as "Joy's law." This feature may play an important part in the exchange of hemispheric polarities. H. Babcock's well-known theory of solar magnetic activity (1961) states that as a cycle progresses, fragments of the magnetic concentrations from decayed groups are carried toward the Sun's poles by a flow of gases within the intergranular network.

Since magnetic fragments from the trailing spot begin their travel at a slightly greater latitude, they should reach their destination earlier than leading polarities. As they near the polar regions the rising magnetic concentrations encounter fragments of opposite polarity and cancel them out. According to this hypothesis, the original field eventually disappears, new-cycle polarities build up, and hemispherical reversal occurs.

Another explanation of this process cites the Coriolis effect as a contributing cause of reversal. According to this scenario differential rotation stretches and winds the original north-south (poloidal) field, creating a more concentrated and strengthened east-west (toroidal) field. Since a magnetic field in a plasma tends to push aside the electrically charged ions that make up the highly ionized outer regions of the Sun, that volume, or "rope" of gas becomes more buoyant than its surroundings. As the toroidal field strengthens, the magnetic flux fields grow more buoyant and sections rise to the surface.

The Coriolis effect imparts a twisting motion on the rising fields—clockwise in the north and counter-clockwise in the south. (The same effect causes similar flows around low pressure systems in the Earth's atmosphere.) After the fields become tightly twisted at the equator, the motion of the plasma, coupled with the Coriolis effect, allows the magnetic fields to begin to unwrap. As the toroidal field rises it unwinds completely and regains a poloidal component opposite to the previous field. Eventually the magnetic fields at the poles reverse and a new cycle begins with opposite polarity.

Babcock cited the effects of differential rotation on the Sun's magnetic flux fields as the likely cause of the sunspot cycle and the butterfly pattern. However, such theories build on the long-held assumption that the Sun has a relatively simple magnetic field like the Earth's—basically, one similar to that of a magnetized iron bar. But we must remember the prophetic words of G. E. Hale to the effect that we understand far less about the Sun than popularly believed.

The pass over the Sun's South Pole carried out by the Ulysses probe during the latter part of 1994 has certainly reinforced Hale's words. Several months after Ulysses began its South Pole flyover, scientists at the European Space Agency (ESA) space research and technology center in Noordwijk (the Netherlands) reported that the polar region displayed unexpected magnetic and dynamic characteristics, indicating that our thinking on the magnetic structure of the Sun may need to be revised.

The Sun's magnetic field

The first things that surprised the scientists were the unexpectedly low cosmic radiation activity above the South Pole, and the unexpected uniformity of the Sun's magnetic field. Dr. Richard Marsden, ESA's project scientist explained, "We expected that we were going to find a local increase in the solar field's intensity. But the probe did not detect any such thing and all the evidence so far seems to suggest that the Sun has no south magnetic pole."

The way Ulysses sees the Sun's magnetic field is different from the way it is seen from Earth. Measurements from Earth show the Sun having a magnetic field with magnetic poles that are not the same as the Sun's North and South Poles; as the Sun rotates, the magnetic poles go around. Ulysses, however, found a uniform magnetic field at the Sun and did not detect any magnetic poles.

Could it be that the Sun has a uniform magnetic field? This and other thought-provoking questions are being studied by the team of scientists working on the project, who are keenly looking forward to comparing these results with those that will become available when Ulysses passes over the Sun's north geographic pole in 1995.

However, it is already manifestly clear that the structure of the solar magnetic field in the southern polar region is not as predicted by the traditional models. In particular, the instruments on board Ulysses also detected a new type of very slowly varying electromagnetic waves, with oscillation periods of 10 to 20 hours. The experts' theory is that this is due to an unexpected phenomenon that conveys the solar magnetic field into space through the solar wind.

It is still far too early to say what effect these new findings will have on our overall understanding of the Sun and the interplanetary wind it generates. A vast volume of data running into thousands of millions of bits—all of it of great scientific value—has been acquired during Ulysses' initial polar pass. A detailed analysis will require many months, but one thing is certain: there is no doubt of the complexity of the phenomena that have been observed, which involve the

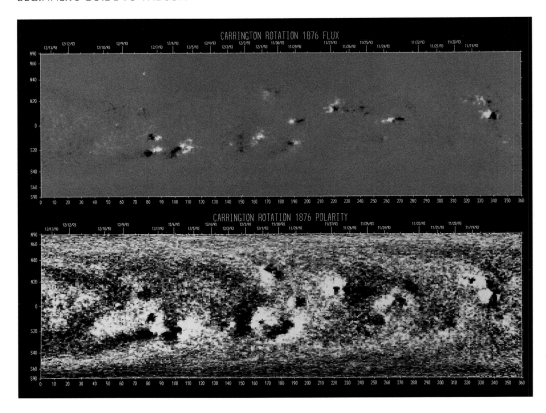

A Kitt Peak Solar Magnetic Field Synoptic Map. Daily full-disk solar magnetograms can be processed by computer into solar rotation maps. Maps like this one correspond to a single solar rotation of the sunspot zone according to a method described by Richard Carrington in 1853. In the upper panel, bright areas represent positive polarities while dark zones are negative. Note the opposite "leading" (more westerly) polarity for sunspot groups in the Northern and Southern Hemispheres of the Sun. Northern leaders normally possess positive polarity during odd-numbered cycles, and southern leaders are negative, a feature which reverses each sunspot cycle. *Photograph courtesy of F. Recely, National Solar Observatory/Kitt Peak.*

combined effects of the solar wind, magnetic field, electromagnetic waves, and fast-moving bursts of particles. Further insights will probably be gained when Ulysses passes over the Sun's North Pole in 1995 and if the mission is extended, when it makes two further polar passes in 2000 and 2001 during a period of increased magnetic activity.

Types of sunspot groups

As we know, the magnetic nature of sunspots was discovered by Hale and others at the famous Mount Wilson Solar Observatory in Southern California. Hale noticed that when a group of spots was centered on the entry slit of his spectroscope, certain spectral lines were separated into multiple components. Moreover, their appearance strongly resembled laboratory spectra that had been subjected to a magnetic field. This phenomenon (newly uncovered when Hale began his research) has come to be known as the Zeeman effect after its discoverer, Dutch physicist Pieter Zeeman, who was awarded the Nobel Prize for his discovery in 1904.

The invention of the magnetograph by Babcock in the 1950s greatly improved upon and extended Hale's early measurements. However, the Mount Wilson system continues to be successfully employed today, even though it was developed over 70 years ago. Hale's classification scheme employs the first three letters of the Greek alphabet, α (alpha), β (beta), and γ (gamma), to identify groups with different magnetic characteristics.

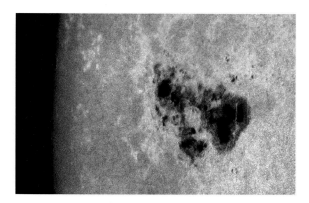

Large patches of faculae can be seen in this photograph of a large sunspot group as it nears the Sun's limb. J. Dragesco obtained this fine photograph near the maximum of solar cycle 22 from a station located in the South of France.

An alpha group is defined as a single unipolar spot or small cluster of spots with the same magnetic polarity. (In practice a few bits of opposite polarity are occasionally found within these groups, but they can generally be ignored.)

Beta groups are composed of distinct leading and trailing sunspots that contain opposite polarities in magnetic balance. This simple, magnetically bipolar sunspot group forms the core of the Mount Wilson system. Hale and his colleagues at Mount Wilson felt that all other clusters were simply variations of this fundamental type.

Gamma groups form the third basic class. They carry mixed polarities within a single, generally large, penumbra. Gamma spot clusters frequently have significantly larger areas than those of the alpha group, but otherwise are similar visually.

A final class, the delta (δ) configuration, was added to the Mount Wilson system by scientists at the National Oceanic and Atmospheric Administration. This label is appended to any

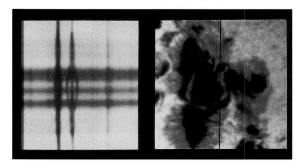

Complex sunspot taken at the National Solar Observatory, Kitt Peak. The vertical black line in the spectrum indicates the slit position of the Zeeman effect. Zeeman splitting of the iron 5250.2 Å line indicates a record field strength of 4130 Gauss (observation was made July 4, 1974, with the McMath Solar Telescope). The white-light photograph shows a sinuous light bridge, which divides the spots' umbra into different magnetic polarities. Twenty minutes before the photo was taken, a major white-light flare occurred. *Photograph courtesy of NOAO/National Solar Observatory.*

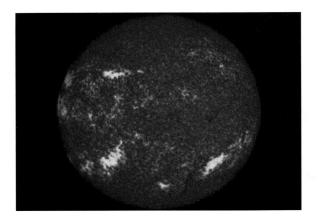

This image shows the full solar disk in a narrow color band in the blue part of the solar spectrum, and it reveals features in the lower atmospheric level of the chromosphere. The exact part of the spectrum used in this image is an absorption line formed by the element calcium called the calcium K line; calcium ions absorb and emit light in this narrow blue band (line). The image shows sunspots and active regions as intense brightenings which are called plage. The surface of the quiet Sun away from sunspots is also covered with a pattern of plage. It is known that the positions of the plage correspond to positions of regions of magnetic fields, and it is thought that somehow the magnetic field is responsible for heating the plage regions, making them brighter. *Photograph courtesy of National Solar Observatory/Sacramento Peak.*

basic group class when spots of mixed magnetic polarity are located within 2 degrees of one another within a single penumbra. The delta classification was added to the Mount Wilson categories because of the especially high incidence of solar flares in groups that have opposite magnetic polarities mixed together.

Since so many of the Sun's active phenomena are rooted in magnetic effects that can be measured, a second type of magnetic cycle can be identified. This effect essentially follows the regular solar cycle, but peaks a little after sunspot maximum. Our old friend Richard Carrington began a series of measurements known as Carrington rotations, which number each revolution of the sunspot zone as it appears from the Earth according to a set period of 27.2753 days. Two-dimensional magnetic maps (synoptic maps) showing these features can be generated for each Carrington rotation, and a total average magnetic flux computed for each diagram. Such maps show that a fivefold increase in flux occurs between spot cycle minimum and maximum, a far larger change than the variation in solar 10.7-centimeter radio flux. Since both the magnetic and 10-centimeter flux reach a peak after sunspot maximum, the magnetic flux is closer in pattern to the radio flux than it is to sunspot number.

Faculae

Sunspot groups are frequently accompanied by bright cloud-like features located a few hundred kilometers above the photosphere, the photospheric faculae. Faculae are glowing clouds of emission that occur where a strong magnetic field creates extra heat (about 300 K degrees above surrounding areas). Faculae are easily seen in white light and were regularly recorded by Galileo and other early solar astronomers. Because of an increased contrast due to limb darkening, they are more easily seen near the limb but occur all across the Sun, even in very high latitudes where they are referred to as polar faculae.

The numbers of sunspot-associated and polar faculae vary with the sunspot cycle; sunspot faculae are more numerous at cycle maximum, whereas polar faculae occur most frequently during the ascending branch of a cycle. The polar faculae turned out to be instrumental in the original mapping of differential rotation in high latitudes, because sunspots are seldom found there and thus cannot be used as measuring posts.

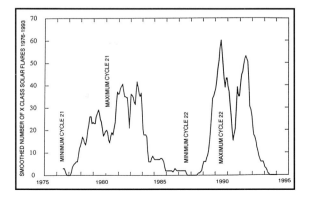

Figure 5.3. The smoothed number of class X solar flares during cycles 21 and 22 (1976–1993). *Diagram courtesy of R. J. Thompson.*

Plage

Plage is a feature also found in the vicinity of virtually all active sunspot groups. This bright phenomenon occurs on a larger scale than faculae and is especially visible in spectroheliograms and similar observations—particularly those in the calcium II, or K line. Plages are extended emission features that appear as the first magnetic flux pierces the photosphere, and last until the magnetic fields merge with the background. They are similar to faculae but are nearly always brighter and more extensive. In fact, a majority of a typical active area is taken up by plage, not sunspots. Curiously, spicules (see Chapter 6) are never seen over plage, but they frequently surround it. This may be due to the considerable atmospheric heating that takes place in the plage.

Solar flares

And now we turn to one of Nature's most impressive events, the cataclysmic energy releases we call solar flares. Solar flares are sudden eruptions of energy in the Sun's atmosphere which last for minutes to hours, and from which radiation and particles are emitted. (Flares typically begin their eruption in the lower corona, but since they are closely tied to magnetic fields above sunspots, we discuss them in this chapter.)

Solar flares occur when strong magnetic fields—almost, but not always above sunspot groups—get wound up in tight spirals and suddenly break apart. Such a field apparently erupts, reconnects, and simplifies. Two destabilization scenarios are thought possible. In one, the field is subject to increasing twist until it reaches a critical state beyond which it becomes unstable. Then electric current sheets form, and the field dissipates rapidly into heat and motion.

In the other explanation, strongly twisted magnetic fields are a necessary but not sufficient condition for flaring, and some external perturbation is required for destabilization (for example, see Chapter 6). Whatever the exact process, vast amounts of energy in the form of heat, radiation, and massive clouds of electrically charged particles explode into the solar environment. During a major solar flare the amount of energy released into interplanetary space can equal the combined explosive power of 20,000 million million tons of TNT!

The number of flares varies in concert with the sunspot cycle, although the largest frequently occur either a little before or up to two years after the sunspot peak. They are particularly likely to erupt along magnetic inversion lines (inversion lines separate regions of opposing magnetic polarity within solar active areas), and in complex spot groups where strong magnetic polarities are mixed and located in close proximity.

Flares are classified on the basis of both their area at the peak brightness in Hα light, and according to their X-ray output. Optical flare observations are made at numerous observatories scattered around the globe. The brightness Importance scale is based on flare area, as outlined below:

Importance 0 (sub-flare): ≤ 2.0 square degrees
Importance 1: 2.1–5.1 square degrees
Importance 2: 5.2–12.4 square degrees
Importance 3: 12.5–24.7 square degrees
Importance 4: ≥ 24.8 square degrees

One square degree on the Sun is equivalent to a little over 147 million square kilometers, so flares can be much larger than the Earth. A brightness qualifier F, N or B is frequently appended to the importance character to indicate faint, normal or bright (for example, Importance 3B).

Solar flares are also ranked by their maximum X-ray energy output in the 1 to 8 angstrom range, as measured by sensors on board the Geostationary Operational Environmental Satellites (GOES). Each class is defined according to the maximum intensity (I) of the energy received at the detector per square centimeter per second.

class B: $I < 10^{-3}$ erg cm^{-2} s^{-1} class M: $10^{-2} \leq I < 10^{-1}$ erg cm^{-2} s^{-1}
class C: $10^{-3} \leq I < 10^{-2}$ erg cm^{-2} s^{-1} class X: $I \geq 10^{-1}$ erg cm^{-2} s^{-1}

Flares are frequently accompanied by bursts of radio emission in wavelengths from centimeters to dekameters. The emissions (designated as Type I-V bursts) may be in the form of sweeps, noise storms which last from a few hours to days, or in bursts, which can also be relatively long-lived but are more often measured in minutes. Type II bursts occur in loose association with major flares and are indicative of a shock wave moving out through the solar atmosphere. Occasionally, a major flare emits significant numbers of protons. Such events—known as proton flares—can have a major impact on the terrestrial environment.

A new measurement of flare activity, the X-ray Region Index (XRI), was developed recently by Patrick McIntosh at the National Oceanic and Atmospheric Administration's Space Environment Laboratory in Boulder, Colorado. This index is a measure of the cumulative X-ray intensity of class M and X flares produced in a particular sunspot group. In calculating a region's XRI, a class M1.0 flare counts as 0.1, an X1.0 as 1.0, an X3.2 as 3.2, and so forth.

For example, if a group spawns six flares at the class M or greater level—an M1, two M2's, An X1, an X5 and an X6—the group's XRI would be 0.1 + 2(0.2) + 1 + 5 + 6, or 12.3. Since the number and intensity of flares varies with the sunspot cycle and among individual spot groups, a different type of butterfly diagram can be constructed from the X-ray index. Figure 5.12 illustrates this feature of solar activity during a large portion of cycle 22.

Advances in solar observation

One of the more interesting and exciting aspects of the current astronomical scene is the ability of advanced space technology to provide information about some of the more exotic ramifications of solar and stellar phenomena. Special techniques have radically altered the science of astronomy, especially in the ways the universe is viewed and research is conducted.

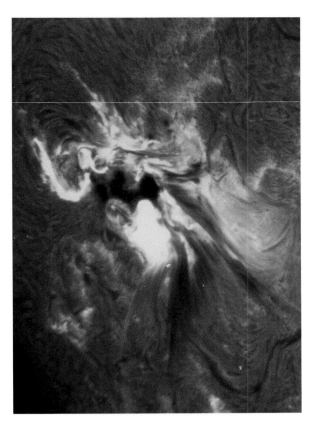

A huge solar flare erupts in NOAA/USAF Region 5395 on March 9, 1989. *Photograph courtesy of T. Compton.*

A graphic example of this sophisticated approach to data gathering was recently announced by NASA. In April 1991 the space shuttle *Atlantis* deployed the Compton Gamma Ray Observatory, a project developed and managed by Goddard Space Flight Center in Greenbelt, Maryland. Since that time, radiation sensors aboard the Compton Observatory have obtained an extraordinary amount of information about the gamma-ray sky, much of which can be processed by computer into images that closely resemble photographs.

The work is performed by the Energetic Gamma Ray Experiment Telescope and Imaging Compton Telescope. Operation of the instruments is a cooperative effort by the Max Planck Institute for Extraterrestrial Physics in Germany and the University of New Hampshire. Normally these instruments collect data from stellar and extragalactic sources. However, when the situation calls for it—during the eruption of an intense solar flare, for instance, or when unusually high solar activity is predicted—the equipment can be commanded to direct its attention toward the Sun. The Compton Telescope is capable of observing flare activity in two modes: imaging, and burst. When the equipment is alerted to a strong flare, the telescope mode is readjusted so that solar neutron events carry a high priority in the data collection process. Meanwhile, the burst mode continually integrates gamma-ray spectra from two detector modules. One operates in the low 0.1 to 1.0 megaelectronvolt (MeV) range, and the other in the high energy, 1 to 10 MeV arena. The system is capable of detecting upward and downward motion, and of separating gamma rays from neutrons through analyses of their electron or proton energy loss.

Solar flare associated with gamma rays have been monitored from satellites since the early 1970s, but only in the high-energy range. Gamma-ray spectra were first detected in the great flares that occurred in August 1972 by an instrument designed by E. L. Chupp of the University of New Hampshire, and flown on the OSO-7 spacecraft. In the period 1980 through 1989, a number of events were detected with the Gamma Ray Spectrometer aboard the Solar Maximum Mission satellite. However, for a variety of reasons imaging gamma-ray telescopes had never been directed toward the Sun.

Several years ago, NASA's Compton Observatory began to fill this void by collecting data on many such events. The effects spawned by the powerful class X flares that occurred in Sunspot Region 6659 in June 1991 are especially intriguing. During this unusual opportunity, the spacecraft was reoriented and its instruments configured into the imaging mode, eliminating the need for an automated response to the dramatic surge in activity.

Three class X solar flares were observed by Compton Observatory instruments during June. These were extremely intense phenomena, ranked from X10 to X12+. (X12 is the most powerful X-ray class for a flare event. Flares exceeding this intensity swamp the GOES sensors.) The events that occurred on June 9 and 11 were observed near their start, since both erupted during orbital sunrise. Because of orbital constraints, observations of the June 15 flare began 50 minutes after the event began.

The impulsive stages of the flares, which occurred on the 11th and 15th, were followed by

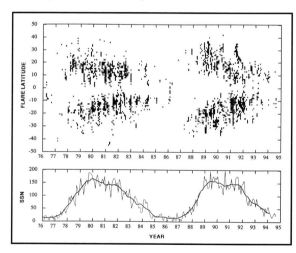

Figure 5.4. This is an example of a butterfly diagram showing the location of energetic flares that originated in sunspot regions during the period extending from 1976 until September 1994. The diagram is based on class M or X flares during that interval, with a grey-scale determined by the number and energy (the X-ray Region Index—see text) of the flares occurring during each calendar month. For comparison, the variation of the monthly (thin line) and the yearly smoothed sunspot number (thick line) are shown on the lower graph with identical timescale. *Diagram courtesy of R. J. Thompson, IPS Radio & Space Services.*

a spectacular gamma ray "afterglow," which lasted for more than 5 hours after the first event, and for more than 90 minutes after the June 15 flare.

One explanation for this phenomenon ties the long afterglow to protons raised to extremely high energies by the flare explosion and stored in a series of magnetic loops—a type of coronal arcade or "magnetic slinky"—in the solar atmosphere. If this theory is correct protons are stored at the Sun in a manner similar to the way they are in the Earth's Van Allen radiation belts. On the Sun, however, they slowly escape, causing the long-lasting glow observed by the Compton instruments. Such a scenario could substantially increase our knowledge of the behavior of particles in the solar environment.

The Compton Observatory also secured the first image of any celestial object taken in the "light" of neutrons. The neutrons were released in nuclear collisions at the Sun produced by especially intense flare eruptions and spewed outward into space. When they arrived at the Compton Observatory, the neutrons produced flashes of light that were recorded by photomultipliers in the project and eventually computer-processed into images.

6
The Sun's Atmosphere

More than 300 years ago, English astronomer and physicist Sir Isaac Newton discovered that by passing sunlight through a glass prism it could be split into its basic colors: red, orange, yellow, green, blue, indigo, and violet. Today, we call this range of light the visible spectrum, since the human eye is sensitive only to this specific band of solar radiation.

As we mentioned in Chapter 2, at the beginning of the 19th century, when a narrow slit was introduced into Newton's experiment, a magnified solar spectrum revealed hundreds of fine dark lines (each an image of the slit) superimposed on the familiar spectral background. These are known as Fraunhofer lines after their primary discoverer. Some 50 years later scientists learned that under certain conditions each chemical element produces its own individual pattern of spectral lines. Such features can appear as dark absorption lines or as bright emission lines, which show that the source is a transparent gas radiating with high emissivity. (That is, the atoms are excited to a high-energy state and release photons as they gradually dissipate energy.)

Each set of spectral lines is unique to a specific element, just as our fingerprints are unique to us. By studying such lines we can determine the chemical makeup, temperature, and density of celestial bodies—information that cannot be obtained from normal photographs. In fact, spectroscopy is responsible for many of the 20th century's greatest astronomical discoveries.

Ask a child to color a picture of the Sun and you'll probably be rewarded with a big yellow ball. That's natural, since the Sun does appear to be yellow when all its visible radiation, the colors deep violet through dark red, are mixed and seen through our eyes. We call this blend white, or integrated, light. We have learned a great deal about the Sun through spectroscopy, especially about the solar atmosphere, for unless it is studied with special instruments, it remains hidden from normal view by the brilliant glow of the photosphere and a weak emission in white light due to its low density. The single exception occurs during a total solar eclipse, when the Sun's inner and outer atmospheres spring dramatically into view.

The lowest portion of the Sun's extended atmosphere is known as the chromosphere. The chromosphere lies above the photosphere and beneath the transition zone and outer solar atmosphere, or corona. The transition zone is the very narrow region of the solar atmosphere that separates the chromosphere and corona, where the temperature rises sharply from 20,000 to nearly a million Kelvin degrees. During a total solar eclipse the chromosphere appears twice—as the advancing lunar limb first covers the solar disk, and at the end of totality just before the Moon starts to uncover the Sun. Without optical assistance we see the chromosphere at totality as a thin red rim encircling the Sun.

The chromosphere

The solar chromosphere and several solar prominences are visible in this photograph of the July 1991 total solar eclipse. *Photograph courtesy of A. S. Landry.*

It is a relatively simple task to record the spectrum of the chromosphere during an eclipse, and much of our early knowledge of this region was acquired this way. C. A. Young first recorded the chromospheric spectrum using a spectroscope at the eclipse of 1870. The flash spectrum, so named because it appears only briefly, is composed of bright emission lines and faint optical radiation that roughly match the Fraunhofer absorption spectrum, the difference lying mainly in intensity. Although Young employed a conventional spectroscope for his measurements, he correctly suggested that the same record could be made by using a slitless spectroscope with the thin sliver of chromosphere itself forming the slit. For many years now even better information has been obtained with a close relative of the spectroscope, the spectrohelioscope, which can produce a picture of the chromosphere extending right across the face of the Sun. More recently, special narrow-band filters have been developed that simplify and improve such images.

The distinctive color of the chromosphere is due almost entirely to the element hydrogen, which makes up a substantial portion of its chemical makeup. This is also the key to the special filters, which typically show the Sun within the isolated light of one of hydrogen's principal spectral lines, a wavelength in the red portion of the spectrum known as the hydrogen-alpha line. Such filters block all other radiation and allow us to observe and photograph many solar features directly.

The density of the chromosphere declines dramatically with height: the amount of overlying gases decreases by a factor of 100 in the first 500 kilometers of altitude. By comparison, the total amount of air in our atmosphere drops by a factor of 2 in the first 8 kilometers above the Earth.

As you might suspect, the temperature of the chromosphere also declines with height, but only for a time. At altitude of about 500 kilometers the temperature of the chromosphere drops to a minimum of about 4400 K degrees. The temperature then begins to rise until we enter the lower reaches of the Sun's outer atmosphere, where it reaches an incredible 1,000,000 to 2,000,000 K degrees. None of the

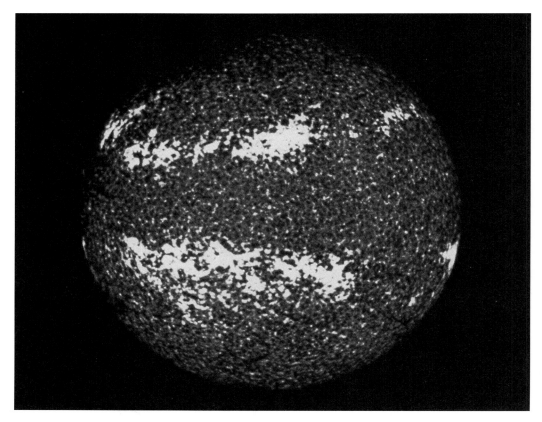

This calcium K spectroheliogram shows the mottled Sun indicative of magnetic activity in the chromospheric network. *Photograph courtesy of the National Optical Astronomy Observatories.*

current chromospheric models really explains this region of the Sun's atmosphere, however, and some studies suggest that the chromosphere's minimum temperature could be as much as 25 percent lower than currently believed.

To summarize, we see that the chromosphere is made up of a relatively thin layer of ordinary solar gases that are raised above the sun and blanket it. In spectroheliograms we find that the chromosphere is composed of a coarsely mottled configuration of bright knots of material known as the chromospheric network, which is especially visible when taken in the Calcium II K band. The chromospheric thickness is variable, extending to about 8000 kilometers above the photosphere. Its density and temperature decline as we move outward, but the temperature reverses direction and begins to increase rapidly after a few hundred kilometers. Before we leave the chromosphere let's take a quick look at some emarkable features of the Sun's inner atmosphere: fibrils and spicules.

Fibrils and Spicules

Fibrils can be seen as sinuous structures similar to the pattern produced by iron filings in a magnetic field, and they are in fact aligned along solar magnetic fields.

They are more prominent near sunspot groups, where they seem to embrace the cluster's central umbrae, but they can be seen all over the Sun's surface. Fibrils typically appear as dark features but often have bright roots that indicate higher temperatures at their bases. Frequently, plagettes (small bright patches containing strong magnetic elements, which congregate along supergranule boundaries) are seen near conspicuous concentrations of fibrils.

Spicules are also features of the chromosphere. When viewed along the limb, their appearance has been compared to that of a burning prairie. Although they are considered small features on the gargantuan scale of the Sun, spicules can

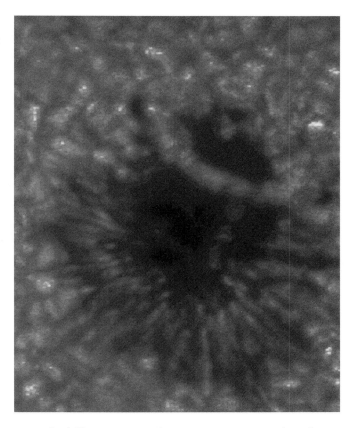

Penumbral filaments around a sunspot group near the solar limb, as shown in the Hα absorption line. *Photograph courtesy of the National Solar Observatory/Sacramento Peak.*

reach out radially to heights greater than the diameter of the Earth. When viewed through special movies, spicules appear as clusters of tiny flames flickering in and out of existence on time-scales of only a few minutes.

When seen projected against the Sun's disk in the light of atomic hydrogen, however, they appear dark, like fibrils. Spicules do not cover the entire chromospheric surface. Rather, they seem to clump together in hedgelike structures. Therein lies what may be their real importance, since studies indicate that beneath each group of spicule "bushes," near their hot, bright bases, lies a strong magnetic concentration. Understanding the role such phenomena play in the chromosphere and elsewhere has become an important part of current solar research.

Prominences and filaments

Higher up, rooted in the photosphere but extending through the chromosphere and into the corona, we find prominences and filaments, among the most strikingly beautiful of all solar phenomena. These are a highly diverse group of features; in reality, just about any cloud of material raised above the solar surface can

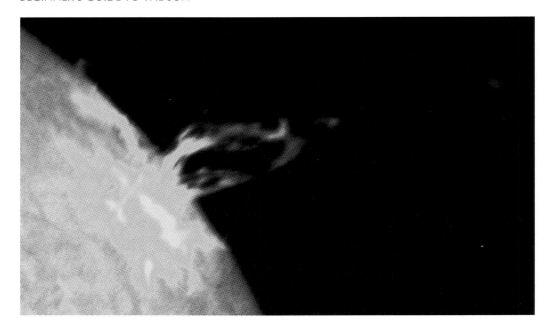

An eruptive prominence, seen in Hα on June 20, 1989. Prominences that suddenly lift off from the Sun are called eruptive. Material from the upper parts of the eruption may escape into interplanetary space, while the matter (hydrogen gas) in the lower brightest parts of the loop usually streams downward. *Photograph courtesy of the National Optical Astronomy Observatories.*

be called a prominence. When they are present, prominences can easily be seen along the Sun's limb during a total eclipse. These structures are also tinged with the telltale reddish glow that indicates large amounts of hydrogen.

Prominences have been observed for centuries. A chronicle from a Russian monastery recorded in May 1185 states, "the Sun became like a thin crescent of the moon, from the horns of which a glow similar to that of red-hot charcoals was emanating. It was terrifying for Man to see this sign of the Lord." Heady stuff!

Since for centuries prominences could only be observed when the Moon had totally eclipsed the Sun, they were long thought to be a type of cloud or other feature of the Moon's atmosphere. Eventually, however, at about the time the sunspot cycle was confirmed (1851), Swedish scientists determined that these phenomena failed to move with the Moon and thus belonged to the Sun. Prominences assume many forms but can be divided into two basic categories: quiescent and active (eruptive).

Quiescent prominences are long-lived, mammoth structures that rise to heights of many thousands of kilometers above the Sun. They are supported by magnetic field loops rising from within the photosphere. During an eclipse they often appear as huge columns of flame jutting outward from the Sun's limb, yet prominences are relatively cool when compared with their surroundings—about 10,000 K degrees. Typically, quiescent prominences are between 100,000 and 600,000 kilometers long and perhaps 7500 kilometers thick.

Many eruptive prominences spend nearly all their lifetimes in the quiescent stage before gradually lifting off the solar surface (erupting) and disappearing. Other types develop much more rapidly and may rise 100,000 kilometers or more above the Sun's surface. They are frequently associated with one of the most powerful solar phenomena, solar flares. Many coronal mass ejections are followed into interplanetary space by the remnants of prominence eruptions.

Filaments are prominences seen projected against the solar disk. They too sometimes become detached and leave the Sun, and when this occurs they are called disappearing solar filaments. For some time astronomers believed that such events caused geomagnetic disturbances. Current thinking casts these phenomena as more likely merely indicators of magnetic instabilities on the Sun. Thus the role they play in terrestrial disturbances may, like that of their limb brethren, be limited to an association with coronal mass ejections. However, filaments also serve an important secondary function, since they trace out points on the solar surface where the radial magnetic field vanishes—the inversion lines that separate regions of opposite magnetic polarity we touched on in Chapter 5.

The following outline, used by Big Bear Solar Observatory astronomer Harold Zirin, is a good example of the many classification schemes for solar prominences:

Quiescent:
a) prominences or filaments in or near active regions
b) prominences or filaments in quiet regions
c) ascending prominences (once long-lived)

Active:
a) limb events
b) loops and coronal rain
c) surges; collimated ejected material previously not seen
d) sprays; uncollimated ejecta previously visible as pre-flare elevated features.

The corona

We now come to the Sun's outer atmosphere—the corona. The corona is an extraordinarily hot, extremely thin portion of the Sun's atmosphere extending outward from the chromosphere-transition zone. The high temperature of the corona accounts for its huge extent and strongly implies that most of its atoms are ionized, particularly

A field of spicules on the surface of the Sun in red Hα light. A spicule is a short-lived (minutes) narrow jet of gas spouting out of the solar chromosphere. *Photograph courtesy of the National Optical Astronomy Observatories.*

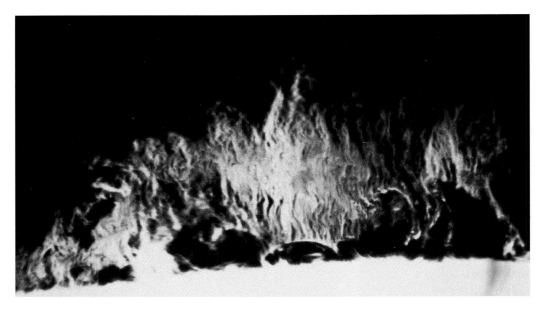

A delicate quiescent prominence of the Sun, about 50,000 kilometers high. *Photographed in Hα light at the National Solar Observatory, Sacramento Peak, New Mexico.*

the hydrogen atoms that make up about 90 percent of the solar atmosphere. The corona is, therefore, largely a swarm of electrified particles. (When the Ulysses spacecraft passed above the Sun's equator in March 1995, scientists conducted a coronal sounding experiment, in which they used the spacecraft's radio beam to measure the electron content of the Sun's corona.)

During a total solar eclipse the corona appears as a spectacular but ghostlike apparition composed mainly of long irregular streamers that seem to reach into space for a million kilometers or more, and portions of the corona actually do extend outward for many solar diameters. Nowadays astronomers can regularly observe a portion of the corona with an instrument called a coronagraph, which creates an artificial eclipse by covering the bright photosphere with a saucerlike plate called an occulting disk. Good coronagraphs can detect the corona out to nearly 1.5 solar radii.

What is the source of the corona's pearly white light? The corona consists of a very hot gas strewn with protons and free electrons (electrons which are not bound to any atom). Out to about 700,000 kilometers from the photosphere, the coronal light we see during an eclipse (the K corona) is simply sunlight from the photosphere that is bounced about by these electrified particles. The K corona's surface brightness varies with the solar cycle, becoming about 50 percent greater at maximum. No dark absorption lines appear in the spectrum of the K corona because the very high speeds of its component electrons cause the lines to broaden into the continuous spectrum.

Interplanetary dust grains rather than electrons play a dominant role in the appearance of coronal light as we move out beyond 1.5 or 2 solar radii and

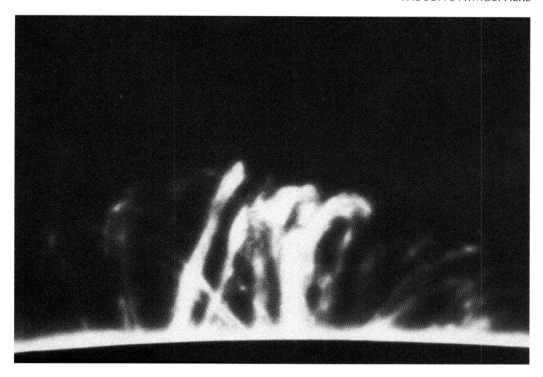

Here we see a set of prominences resembling loops. Often in prominences material is seen to drain down the prominence and fall into the Sun. This material is called coronal rain. It somehow cools from the surrounding hot corona, condenses on the prominence, and falls to the surface of the Sun. Exact details of this process are still unknown. *Photograph courtesy of the National Solar Observatory/Sacramento Peak.*

gradually merge into the F, or Fraunhofer, corona. The effect here is similar to one most of us have seen before—the light-scattering by tiny dust particles floating in a beam of sunlight that renders them visible.

The F corona extends far beyond the Earth into space, so far that it can actually be seen at night as a faint glow along the ecliptic (the plane of Earth's orbit around the Sun). Such zodiacal light is especially visible from low latitudes, but can occasionally be spotted at high latitudes. Since the dust particles in the F corona move much slower than the electrons in the K corona, absorption lines (similar in pattern to those of the photosphere) do appear in its spectrum.

If the corona were a dense mass of plasma its tremendous temperature would immediately incinerate all life on Earth. However, since it is very rarefied—nearer a perfect vacuum than most vacuum pumps on the Earth can produce—you could place your hand within its borders and feel no warmth. Not enough particles would come into contact with your skin for you to feel any sensation.

Spectroscopy provided the clues that led to a determination of the temperature of the corona. Until astronomers identified the origin of a few special lines in the coronal spectrum, they generally assumed that the corona was about the temperature of the photosphere (≈5800 K), or perhaps somewhat less. Such views endured for a century after the first serious studies of the corona began in the mid-19th century.

In particular, a line in the green portion of the coronal spectrum did not appear to match any known element. Analyses by German and Swedish spectroscopists at the start of World War II (principally Bengt Edlén) eventually determined that this and similar spectral lines were caused by extraordinarily ionized atoms (atoms stripped of some or all of their electrons) of iron, nickel, and calcium. For atoms to become this ionized, temperatures of between 1,000,000 and 2,000,000 K degrees are required; so the corona must radiate at these vast temperatures. In fact, some years later these findings were verified through sophisticated studies of the Sun's radio emission.

How is the corona heated to such an incredibly high temperature? This is a complex question that astronomers still grapple with. We know the corona's temperature could not be generated by radiation from the 6000 degree photosphere. It is even more mystifying that the corona's temperature increases as we move away from the Sun, which seems to defy logic. Through the years many mechanisms have been proposed to account for this, but the most likely appears to be rooted in a source that has by now become familiar.

As with nearly all solar phenomena, it seems the Sun's magnetic structure lies at the center of this question. The corona is known to be a violently turbulent region filled with a variety of magnetic phenomena. Some areas of the corona—those that emit X-rays—are heated to even higher temperatures, up to several million degrees. We do not understand how this localized heating occurs, but many physicists believe the continuous churning of the magnetic fields above sunspots produces electric currents that dissipate in the corona and cause the temperature to rise drastically. Some say the coronal heat is related to the Sun's continual generation of numerous tiny eruptions called nano-, or micro-flares, which occur within the smaller coronal field structures. This source is, however, less likely.

Whatever mechanism eventually accounts for the corona's high temperature, the loop-shaped features of the active corona known as coronal loops, which contain numerous spiral-shaped magnetic fields, are likely to play an important role. Unfortunately, the fine resolution required to study such phenomena is not available with most current X-ray satellites. The heating of the corona is a complicated problem, and to date no clear mechanism has been agreed upon that completely accounts for it.

Solar wind

Several decades ago astronomers struggled with a different problem involving the corona. As with all objects, the influence of the Sun's gravity falls off rapidly as distance increases, so a stable corona could only be maintained by some type of containing force. At one time this restriction was believed to stem from the pressure of interstellar gas—something like liquid surrounding a large bubble. However, calculations soon showed that the high temperature of the corona would easily overwhelm such a weak constraint and allow the farthest reaches of the Sun's atmosphere to continuously expand into space.

In other research at about this same time, some astronomers questioned the notion that the pressure of sunlight caused the tails of comets to continuously point away from the Sun. Soon thereafter it was learned that this tenuous influence would be far too weak to produce such an effect. As an alternative, a few scientists suggested that a more likely cause was a steady outflow of tiny particles streaming away from the Sun.

Unfortunately, any

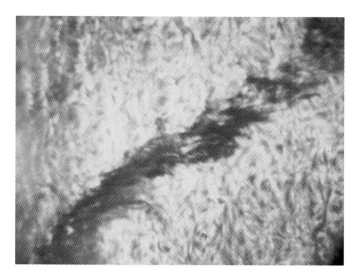

This is a high-resolution image of a filament—a prominence seen projected against the solar disk—in the Hα absorption line. The image is near the limb, and from this angle we can see that the filament appears to rise above the chromosphere by thousands of kilometers. The filament extends into the million degree corona, but represents a cool region with a temperature of only thousands of degrees Kelvin. *Photograph courtesy of the National Solar Observatory/Sacramento Peak.*

such flow of material could not be directly measured from the Earth since it would be deflected by the geomagnetic field. The first hints of a solution came from instruments aboard early Soviet and American satellites, and the issue was eventually resolved in the 1960s after measurements from the U.S. Mariner II spacecraft showed the outflow of particles to be a continuous "solar wind" with a velocity that averages around 300 to 400 kilometers per second. (The Ulysses spacecraft has recently observed that the solar wind emanating from the Sun's southern polar region flows at about double this rate, or around 750 kilometers per second.)

We now realize that the Sun is losing a large amount of mass through this process. Incredible as it may seem, a staggering several million tons of solar material is lost from the Sun each second! No need to worry about our incredibly shrinking Sun, however. It is so large that at this rate it would take over 150,000 million years for the Sun to lose just a small percentage of its present mass.

On the Earth the prevailing winds generally are horizontal to the surface. On the Sun however, the upper atmosphere achieves such enormous temperatures that the solar wind is forced outward with increasing speed. Essentially, the wind blows away from the Sun in all directions and drags with it parts of the solar magnetic field. Thus far the solar wind has been observed by deep-space probes more than 40 times farther away from the Sun than the Earth's orbit.

This superb photograph of the solar corona was obtained at the June 1973 eclipse by a team from the National Center for Atmospheric Research. In order to show a maximum amount of detail, a special camera designed by G. A. Newkirk Jr. was coupled with a radial-density filter, a device that dims the inner coronal brightness much more than the outer corona. *Photograph courtesy of the High Altitude Observatory, National Center for Atmospheric Research.*

Although it is electrically balanced, the solar wind consists almost exclusively of charged particles and is an excellent electrical conductor. The wind is ubiquitous in the Solar System, occupying all of interplanetary space and controlling the space environments of most, if not all, objects within it. For non-magnetic bodies such as Earth's Moon, the solar wind impacts the surface directly. For magnetized bodies such as the Earth, the solar wind and the magnetic field interact to form an enormous magnetic cavity surrounding the body, the magnetosphere.

Coronal holes

As is true for many discoveries, new information in one field often supplies clues to the answers of long-standing questions in another. For nearly a century astronomers suspected that some type of solar source was responsible for certain types of disturbances in the Earth's magnetic field, storms which seemed to occur regularly in concert with the Sun's 27-day rotational rate. The first hint of such phenomena came from an investigation over a half-century ago which suggested that unseen M-regions might be the source of such storms.

The high temperature of the corona causes it to radiate strongly in ultraviolet radiation and soft (low-energy) X-rays. However, atmospheric absorption makes such radiation difficult to detect at the Earth. Consequently, the first detailed images of the corona's structure awaited the X-ray pictures taken from early spacecraft—initially, the U.S. Orbiting Solar Observatory (OSO) satellites. When these images were received they clearly showed large open gaps in the corona.

The presence of these low-density areas, known today as coronal holes, is now regularly monitored with special instruments aboard X-ray imaging satellites such as the Japanese/U.S. Yohkoh spacecraft. These features can also be inferred from ground-based solar images measured at certain wavelengths—observations routinely obtained by monitoring the Helium I 10830Å spectral line at the Vacuum Solar Telescope at Kitt Peak National Solar Observatory. Although they do not always affect the Earth, some coronal holes can cause very high speed "gusts" in the solar wind, which produce geomagnetic storms that recur at regular intervals. The once-mysterious M-regions are mysterious no more.

Coronal holes are closely associated with those regions on the Sun that have what is called an "open" magnetic geometry. That is, the magnetic field lines associated with them extend far outward into interplanetary space, rather than looping back to the photosphere. Ionized material can flow easily along such a path, and this in turn aids the mechanism that causes high speed solar wind streams to develop. Long-lived coronal holes (some of those that form above the Sun's poles may endure for several years) occur primarily during the declining portion of a solar cycle. They form when smaller holes at low solar latitudes join with those above the poles. The situation is different during a cycle's ascent to maximum, when coronal holes are unstable features with short lifetimes characterized by sudden eruptive outflows.

CMEs

We have described how vast amounts of solar material are lost into interplanetary space through the solar wind. But the Sun also loses mass in another, more dramatic way—through the release of quite immense quantities of coronal material into space (up to 11,000 million tons of solar matter in some discharges). Like

This striking view of the solar corona was prepared from data obtained by NASA's Solar Maximum Mission satellite. The prominent feature extending from the Sun towards the west is a coronal spike; others can also be seen to the south of this phenomenon. The spike—or coronal streamer—extending from the densest corona region persists well beyond 1.5 million kilometers from the surface. The white dots, which are camera imperfections, are the approximate size of the Earth. *Photograph courtesy of NASA.*

97

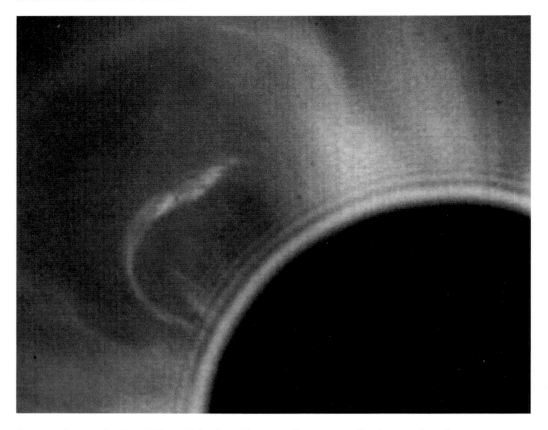

A coronal mass ejection lifting off the Sun. The outer loop—actually the exterior of an enormous bubble of gas—is the leading edge of the CME, while the bright inner loop is an erupting prominence. *Photograph courtesy of A. J. Hundhausen, National Center for Atmospheric Research.*

the solar wind and coronal holes, these expulsions, known as coronal mass ejections, or more simply CMEs, are relative latecomers to solar physics, mainly because CMEs are primarily detectable from spacecraft-mounted coronographs, which employ sensitive electronic detectors in place of photographic film to record them.

CMEs were first observed in 1973 by instruments aboard the U.S. solar satellite OSO-7 and have subsequently been explored from other orbiting platforms such as Skylab, the Naval Research Laboratory P78-1, Solar Maximum Mission and ISEE-3 satellites. These observations have been complemented by others in the inner corona from ground-based instruments at Mauna Loa Solar Observatory in Hawaii, and by the zodiacal-light photometers on board the Helios spacecraft.

Although coronal mass ejections exhibit a number of morphological features, they often appear as giant loops or bubbles of solar material rooted to the photosphere. A more exact definition was provided by National Center for Atmospheric Research astronomer A. J. Hundhausen in 1984: "an observable change in coronal structure that (1) occurs on a time scale between a few minutes and

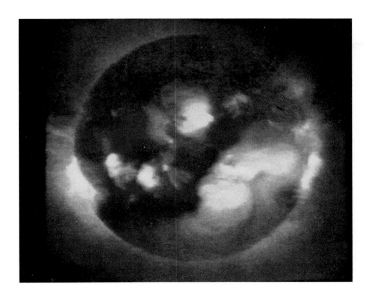

The X-ray corona as it appeared during the end of November 1991. Note the large coronal hole—a low-density area within the solar atmosphere. A long series of extraordinary images like this have been obtained by the Soft X-ray Telescope aboard the Japanese Yohkoh satellite. This instrument was designed and built as a collaboration between the Lockheed Palo Alto Research Laboratory, the National Astronomical Observatory in Japan, and the University of Tokyo, with support from NASA and the Institute for Space and Astronautical Science (Japan).

several hours, and, (2) involves the appearance of a new, discrete, bright, white-light feature in the coronagraph field of view." An extension of this description requires that the event display a predominantly outward motion.

CMEs are mammoth structures that can occupy up to a quarter of the solar limb before lifting off into space, frequently accompanied by the remnants of an erupting prominence, and less often by a strong solar flare. They appear to originate mainly in closed magnetic field regions within the coronal streamer belt and are thought to arise from changes in the large-scale coronal magnetic field.

Solar flares, on the other hand, result more from the reorganization of small but intense fields generally located near active sunspot regions. It is interesting that CMEs can occur in both normal sunspot/flare zones and at much higher solar latitudes. Moreover, their occurrence seems to follow the traditional butterfly pattern—appearance at low heliographic latitudes during cycle minimum ranging to high latitudes around maximum.

It has long been clear that CMEs are unlikely to be a flare-induced phenomenon. While it is true that solar flares accompany a fair portion of these mass ejections, those CMEs usually begin their departure before the flare occurs; a factor which has contributed to some astronomers' belief that CMEs—and not flares—are the crucial link between the solar disturbance, its propagation through the heliosphere, and the effects of these phenomena at the Earth (Table 6.1, page 100). Further evidence of their disassociation lies in the observation that flares occurring with CMEs typically erupt far to one side of the broad-based mass ejection. Of course solar flares occur in much larger numbers than do CMEs, so only a portion of flares are initiated by these events.

The exact cause of CME-related flares is a matter of conjecture. It has been suggested that when some CMEs lift off, segments of the massive bubble containing oppositely directed magnetic fields become elongated and eventually break apart,

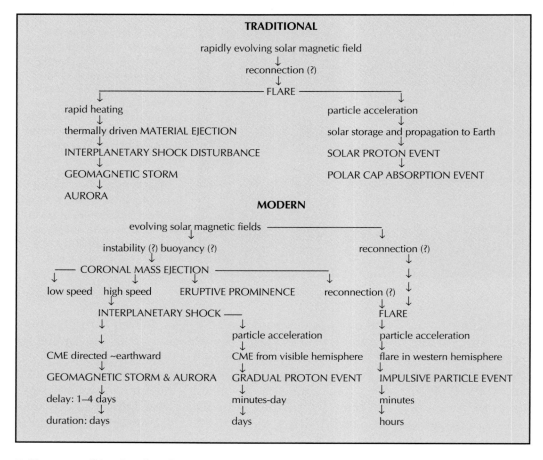

TRADITIONAL

rapidly evolving solar magnetic field
↓
reconnection (?)
↓
——— FLARE ———

rapid heating
↓
thermally driven MATERIAL EJECTION
↓
INTERPLANETARY SHOCK DISTURBANCE
↓
GEOMAGNETIC STORM
↓
AURORA

particle acceleration
↓
solar storage and propagation to Earth
↓
SOLAR PROTON EVENT
↓
POLAR CAP ABSORPTION EVENT

MODERN

evolving solar magnetic fields ———
↓
instability (?) buoyancy (?)   reconnection (?)
↓   ↓
——— CORONAL MASS EJECTION ———
↓   ↓   ↓   ↓   ↓
low speed   high speed   ERUPTIVE PROMINENCE   reconnection (?)   ↓
↓   ↓
INTERPLANETARY SHOCK ———   FLARE
↓   ↓   ↓
↓   particle acceleration   particle acceleration
↓   ↓   ↓
CME directed ~earthward   CME from visible hemisphere   flare in western hemisphere
↓   ↓   ↓
GEOMAGNETIC STORM & AURORA   GRADUAL PROTON EVENT   IMPULSIVE PARTICLE EVENT
↓   ↓   ↓
delay: 1–4 days   minutes-day   minutes
↓   ↓   ↓
duration: days   days   hours

Table 6.1. Traditional and modern paradigms of the chain of events leading to large nonrecurrent geomagnetic storms and their effects. Capital letters depict observational occurrences and lowercase letters indicate physical processes or descriptive characteristics. *This illustration was prepared from a diagram that appeared in a 1993 article by Los Alamos National Laboratory scientist J. Gosling.*

temporarily remaining attached to the Sun. As the fields are distorted and brought together during the ejection, they could reconnect and cause the flare. However, an exact mechanism remains uncertain.

Like flares, the leading edges of fast-moving CMEs, about one third of all these events, drive giant shock waves before them through the solar wind at speeds up to 1200 kilometers per second. (Since they typically move at or below the speed of the solar wind, low-speed CMEs do not drive shock disturbances.) Although flares certainly impart energy to solar particles, CME-initiated shock waves are capable of energizing particles on a much more impressive scale.

As the trailing mass of plasma moves out into interplanetary space it can grow to enormous size. Eventually some of these giant assemblages expand to encompass a greater amount of space than the Sun itself, far larger than the narrow cone covered by outward-moving flare particles.

Locating a Region of the Sun's Invisible Spectrum

Like Sir Isaac Newton, you can use a prism to separate the Sun's light into the primary colors—the band of radiation we call the visible spectrum. But with just a few more materials and a little effort you can detect a portion of the spectrum that is normally invisible—the Sun's infrared radiation.

Materials:
- Large prism
- Several inexpensive thermometers (The experiment can be completed with just one thermometer, but several will make things simpler.)
- Cardboard box, about 60 x 30 x 15 cm deep
- A piece of white cardboard about 30 x 90 cm
- Masking tape, ballpoint pen

Procedure:
Remove the top of the box, and tape the strip of white cardboard inside the box. It will serve as a "projection screen." The screen should curve inward in a gentle arc. Position the prism so that the Sun's spectrum is projected into the box and onto the screen. Mark the ends of the visible spectrum. Next, place the thermometers at equally spaced intervals just beyond the red band. You may need to adjust the thermometer's positions slightly while searching for the highest temperature reading. Remember, because the Earth is rotating you'll only have a limited time to line things up and take your measurements. If a thermometer is placed in the red band, is the temperature higher or lower than the highest reading in the infrared?

Even though its density near the Earth is several million times less than in the inner corona, only a particle or so per cubic centimeter, the coronal solar wind has been found to provide the transportation link in the solar-terrestrial relationship. And as might be suspected, some of its astonishing features profoundly affect the Earth. But more about that in the following chapter.

7

In the Path of the Sun's Emissions

The Sun appears to be a model of consistency, a source of an endless stream of warmth and light. As we have learned, however, it is not as changeless as it seems. The solar-terrestrial environment is the region of space extending from the surface of the Sun out to and including the Earth's magnetic field and parts of its atmosphere. It is a harsh environment dominated by electromagnetic radiation and charged particles from the Sun. The region is subject to dramatic and violent change as events on the Sun blast shock waves, streams of radiation, and energetic particles toward Earth. Despite being far removed from everyday experience, the solar-terrestrial environment has a surprisingly wide and increasing range of effects on modern life.

When solar energy reaches the Earth some eight minutes after leaving the Sun, it heats the atmosphere, surface, and oceans. Most of the infrared (heat) radiation is absorbed as it descends through the atmosphere. In fact if the atmosphere did not absorb this radiation the Earth's temperature could not support most forms of life. Likewise, only a small portion of solar ultraviolet (UV) radiation penetrates the atmosphere since ozone absorbs all but a tiny fraction. Ozone is a form of oxygen made up of three oxygen atoms per molecule. It forms a thin layer in the atmosphere. Once formed however, it can also be destroyed by a range of solar radiation. Just a tiny concentration remains from this process, a portion estimated to be less than 10 parts per million.

The term "ozone hole" is often used to describe a large area of intense ozone depletion that occurs over Antarctica during late August through early October and typically breaks up in late November. The largest hole ever observed occurred on September 27, 1992, when it had an extent of 24.4 million square kilometers.

According to preliminary data obtained by scientists at NASA's Goddard Space Flight Center in Greenbelt, Maryland, the Antarctic ozone hole levels for 1994 were nearly as large and as deep as the record lows. These extremely low levels were recorded by NASA's Total Ozone Mapping Spectrometer aboard the Russian Meteor 3 satellite. They have also been measured by balloon-borne instruments flown from the South Pole, spectrometers on the ground, and an instrument on the US NOAA-9 satellite.

During the years 1992 to 1994 the area of ozone depletion nearly filled the polar vortex wind region that places an upper limit on the possible size of the ozone hole. Scientists have determined that chlorine products from human activities such as electronics and refrigeration are a likely cause of ozone hole formation.

Regardless of whether or not it is naturally occurring, ozone loss has resulted in a 5 to 10 percent increase in UV radiation at several sites in Southern Australia and New Zealand during the last decade, and the effects have been noted among several species of plant and animal life. The amount of ozone varies naturally according to season and latitude, but for more than a decade the seasonal variations have been especially strong.

Most importantly, there appears to have been an overall reduction in the global amount of ozone, particularly over Antarctica, where the amount normally ebbs and flows with the long austral seasons of light and darkness. The thinning ozone layer over Antarctica has caused large plankton kills through overexposure to UV, a consequence which could eventually disrupt the food chain.

Even tiny amounts of UV can cause damage to the body, including sunburn and premature aging of the skin and eventually serious illness. Radiation can also endanger frequent air travelers, primarily those who routinely fly at high altitudes along polar routes, where a thinner atmosphere offers less protection. On a brighter note, UV produces vitamin D, which helps to protect us from some diseases, and of course the rays cause our highly prized suntans.

Several factors influence the ability of the Sun to produce a suntan. The altitude of the Sun (the Earth's thicker atmosphere blocks more radiation when the Sun is low in the sky), the season and time of day, the amount of ozone in the atmosphere, and the individual's personal characteristics all contribute to tanning. The type of UV also plays a role, since shorter wavelengths are far more likely to cause sunburn.

In recent years doctors have discovered that prolonged exposure to UV radiation increases the risk of developing a melanoma, one of the more serious types of skin cancer. In Australia, which has the world's highest rate of this disease, the golden tans which were once so fashionable have given way to a more natural and far safer appearance. But in spite of such attitude changes experts predict more than a million new cases of skin cancer each year.

Even so, small amounts of solar radiation are essential to life. Since all living beings require organic food, the process by which it is formed—photosynthesis— is fundamental to their existence. In fact, living organisms deplete the supply of organic material at a rate such that life on Earth would end after just a few years if this mechanism suddenly ceased. (We actually see photosynthesis slow in the fall when a decreasing amount of sunlight, and consequently a lower production of green chlorophyll, allows the three other major leaf pigments to become more prominent.)

Sunlight transmitted in massless quanta (photons, which carry electromagnetic energy in amounts inversely proportioned to their wavelength), builds carbohydrates and releases oxygen during this complex process chiefly through absorption by molecules of the green plant pigment, chlorophyll. This mechanism has been around for a long time—the remnants of ancient photosynthesis now appear in the form of coal, oil, and natural gas. We can see that these, as well as most of Nature's products, can truly be considered forms of solar energy.

Seasonal Affective Depression Disorder

Is it possible for the Sun to affect us psychologically? An increasing number of scientists think so. Psychologists have identified a disorder they believe is linked directly to the Sun—Seasonal Affective Depression Disorder, or "SADD." In far northern latitudes during extreme winters with little sunlight, millions of people suffer from depression, loss of energy, and anxiety—the symptoms of SADD. Recent estimates indicate that up to 35 million people may suffer from this malady.

SADD has received so much attention in recent years that it has become a major consideration in choosing scientists to work at the South Pole. Researchers believe the disorder is caused by a disruption in our circadian rhythms (the biological clock that controls sleep and is triggered by normal light-dark cycles). The treatment of this ailment is relatively simple—a few hours of "light therapy" each day.

Further evidence of SADD can be found in isolation experiments where test subjects are confined to a small room with no sunlight. These investigations clearly show that circadian rhythms can swing wildly out of synch, resulting in "days" that appear to last for up to 70 hours. Several years ago Stefania Follini spent four months in a New Mexican cave in an experiment designed to test this theory. During her stay Stefania's rhythms became completely disrupted. A telling sidelight of this experiment concerns her decorative choice for her subterranean home—a picture of the Sun hung carefully above her bed.

The magnetosphere

Still, we must travel high above the Earth's surface in order to find the real excitement, to a region of near-space that begins with the upper atmosphere and is sometimes referred to as geospace. Geospace includes the upper portions of the Earth's atmosphere and the outer regions of the Earth's magnetic field, along with materials formed by solar activity. It is here that the Sun's energetic emissions and Earth's magnetic field collide.

In some respects the geomagnetic field is similar to one that would appear if a large bar magnet was placed at the Earth's center. The magnetic axis would then pass through our planet's north and south magnetic poles, extending outward into space with field lines gradually looping around from the north to the south pole. Most of us have seen a two-dimensional demonstration of this pattern when a bar magnet is placed under a sheet of paper covered with iron filings and gently tapped so the bits of metal align themselves with the magnet's invisible field.

However, matter continuously streaming away from the Sun—the quiescent solar wind—distorts the Earth's field into the shape of a giant teardrop known as the magnetosphere. The typical planetary magnetosphere is a magnetic cavity carved out of the solar wind. A planet's dayside magnetosphere is highly compressed in the direction of the Sun by the approaching solar wind and greatly elongated on the nightside (called the antisolar direction). The Earth's magnetosphere contains its internal magnetic field plus the magnetic distortions created by the solar wind. The boundary of the magnetosphere is called the magnetopause, located on the dayside where the magnetic pressure of the Earth's internal field is equal to the net flow pressure of the impinging solar wind.

The unadulterated solar wind does not impinge directly on the magnetopause. Earth's magnetic field is essentially an impenetrable obstacle to the solar wind because of its large electrical conductivity. The supersonic wind must therefore slow down and veer from its original direction in order to flow around the magnetic obstacle ahead. As a result of the required adjustment, a bow-shaped shock wave forms at a fixed distance from the dayside magnetopause.

Along the Earth-Sun line the solar wind slows to subsonic speeds as it crosses the bow shock wave. The space that is outside the magnetopause and inside the bow shock wave is called the magnetosheath—in other words, the magnetosheath contains the deflected solar wind that crosses the bow shock wave and moves downstream outside the magnetopause.

Effects of magnetic storms

Near the maximum of each solar cycle, great storms plague the Earth's magnetic field and dazzling aurorae can be viewed from much lower latitudes than usual. Two important events during the mid-19th century significantly influenced scientific thinking concerning the source of such storms: first, the number of magnetic disturbances was linked to the newly discovered sunspot cycle, and second, English astronomer Richard Carrington observed the first solar flare and suggested it might have some association with a spectacular geomagnetic storm that followed.

Shortly thereafter, evidence began to accumulate that seemed to confirm flares as the source of terrestrial magnetic disturbances. Since then the two phenomena have been reasonably well correlated and the relationship has been generally accepted for more than half a century. In spite of such circumstantial evidence, however, the connection between flares and magnetic storms has never been observed on a one-for-one basis. Some powerful flares, even those centered in the western solar hemisphere where the interplanetary magnetic field should make connection with the Earth most likely, do not result in disturbances, and some storms do not appear to be associated with a particular flare.

The long-standing link between flares and geomagnetic storms is a bit like the story of the boy whose mother sent him to a psychiatrist because he was continually snapping his fingers. "Why do you snap your fingers?" asked the doctor. "To keep the snakes away," countered the boy. "But there are no snakes," argued the doctor. To which the boy replied, "That's because I keep snapping my fingers!"

The flare origin of large geomagnetic storms began to be

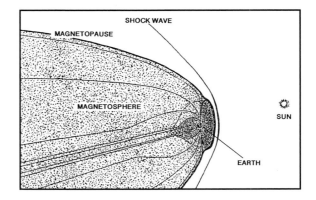

Figure 7.1. A schematic representation of the Earth's magnetosphere. Matter continuously streaming away from the Sun—the solar wind—forms the magnetosphere into a giant teardrop-shaped field that follows the Earth through space.

Aurorae photographed from the Amundsen-Scott Station at the South Pole, Antarctica. *Photograph courtesy of M. Taylor, Loras College.*

called into question nearly two decades ago, when many disturbances were tracked back to the Sun and found to originate with the solar wind and coronal holes. During the ensuing years, storms that repeat at about 27-day intervals—the apparent rotational period of the Sun—were unequivocally tied to these features. (The activity on the Sun that causes recurrent disturbances is not simply the presence of coronal holes, but their variability in concert with magnetic shear and rearrangements of large scale magnetic field structures in the corona.) As we discussed in the previous chapter, such recurrent geomagnetic disturbances take place as matter streaming into space from a low-density portion of the Sun's atmosphere returns to a geoeffective position.

CMEs and storms

Until recently the occurrence of large non-recurrent storms—those often accompanied by the spectacular terrestrial effects we hear described by the media—has continued to be directly linked to the energy bursts from especially violent solar flares, or occasionally to transient coronal holes. Now, however, new evidence has been put forth supporting an alternative theory. This scenario relegates the flares that seem to precede many of these storms to a secondary effect triggered by gigantic ejections of matter from the Sun's atmosphere (see Chapter 6, the section on coronal mass ejections and Table 6.1), and identifies the latter as the true source of all great geomagnetic disturbances. Moreover, this research cites the strength, speed, and configuration of the magnetic fields carried within the ejected material—and not simply energetic solar particles—as the causal agent of all such magnetic storms. Coronal holes and their relationship with the largest flare-productive sunspot regions may play a part in this process. Essentially, the super flare-active regions seem to be associated with peaks of coronal hole areas, especially in the Sun's Southern Hemisphere.

As with most of the Sun's active phenomena, the number of CMEs appears to rise and fall with the solar cycle. Studies show that, on average, the Earth intercepts about six CMEs per month at cycle maximum and less than one for any month around minimum. According to the new research, when the origins of the 37 major and large geomagnetic storms that occurred during the maximum of cycle 21 are analyzed, it appears likely that all but one were associated with the passage of a shock, a CME, or both.

The direction of the looping interplanetary magnetic fields driven by fast CMEs also plays an important role in the new scenario. If the fields point north as the shock and plasma cloud pass the Earth, nothing much happens. The geomagnetic field simply deflects the flow around the magnetosphere. However, when the fields are directed south (opposite to the Earth's field), they reconnect with the terrestrial field, and the possibility of magnetic storms and aurorae rises according to the speed and strength of the rapidly moving flow.

Some very complicated magnetic and electrical processes are then set into motion within and around the magnetosphere. The energy caused by this mechanism drives the ensuing magnetic storm and accelerates both solar and local particles down through the magnetosphere and into the Earth's upper atmosphere where they strike atoms and molecules. When struck, the atmospheric components become excited (ionized, or raised to a higher energy state) and begin to glow.

As most of us know, we call the result aurorae, or northern and southern lights. These beautiful phenomena have been recorded since Aristotle first wrote of them in the fourth century B.C. As circumstances allow this process to occur, huge auroral ovals are formed that ring both magnetic poles. Most auroral activity takes place along this boundary, which expands with increased geomagnetic activity, and not at the poles themselves.

The magnetosphere absorbs and deflects away mainly those particles that carry an electrical

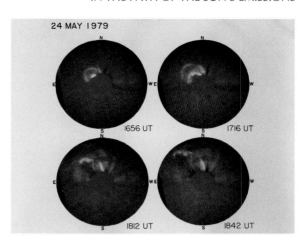

This series of images shows a coronal mass ejection that occurred on May 24, 1979. The images were obtained with a white-light coronagraph experiment called Solwind, which was flown aboard the Air Force Space Test Program satellite P78-1. The experiment imaged the solar corona between March 30, 1979, and September 13, 1985. *Photograph courtesy of R. Howard, Naval Research Laboratory.*

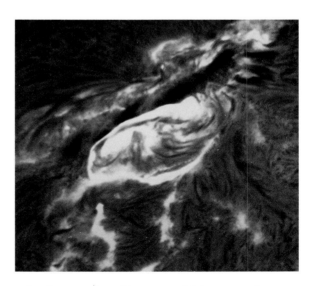

Solar flares such as this event, which occurred on March 14, 1989, strongly influence the radio propagation capabilities of the ionosphere. When, during the eruption of these events, very-low-frequency radio signal variations are displayed graphically, the resulting atmospheric anomalies—known as sudden ionospheric disturbances—produce a distinctive signature. (See Chapter 10.)

107

TABLE 7.1

Some Specific Terrestrial Effects of Solar Activity
- HF Radio Communications—Shortwave Fadeouts in Sunlit Hemisphere
- HF Radio Communications—Degraded Communications During Ionospheric Storms
- HF Radio Communications—Disrupted Communications due to Polar Cap Absorptions
- LF and VLF Communications—Phase Anomalies in Signals
- VHF and UHF Communications—Radio Interference in Sunlit Hemisphere
- VHF and UHF Communications—Unusual Signal Retardation and Refraction in Auroral Zone
- Problems for Over-the-Horizon Radar Systems due to Fadeouts and Ionospheric Disturbances
- Disruption of Geomagnetic Mineral Surveys
- Failure of Power Transmission Grids
- Increased Corrosion in Long Pipelines
- Increased Drag on Satellites
- Failure of Satellite Electronics and Control Systems
- Problems for Navigation Systems
- Hazards to Manned Space Missions
- Hazards to Passengers on High Altitude Aircraft Flights
- Pointing and Operational Problems for Radio Telescopes
- Wide-Spread Sightings of Aurorae
- Clearing Space Debris in Low Orbit
- Production of the Ionosphere, Enabling Long Distance HF Communication
- Increased Production of Stratospheric Ozone?

charge, so the Sun's X-ray and UV radiation pass through it relatively easily. But these rays soon encounter the outer layers of Earth's atmosphere, where most of their energy is dissipated, as we have described. Eventually the remainder descends into the stratosphere and all but a little of the remaining radiation is scattered and absorbed, leaving just enough to support life on the Earth. (Radiation at short wavelengths is more scattered, causing the sky to appear blue.)

In spite of these barriers an especially strong surge of solar activity can cause some spectacular events. (You can see the effects of such activity for yourself by building the simple magnetometer described in the project following this chapter.) As you can see from Table 7.1, examples abound: radio and other types of communications are subject to disruptions, satellites and other spacecraft can go awry, and compass errors near the poles and elsewhere may make aircraft navigation difficult. Even sensitive surveying and mining instruments can be influenced.

Predicting magnetic storms

Our knowledge of the processes that cause these conditions has improved considerably, and we can predict some of them, especially those terrestrial events caused by flare activity (ionospheric disturbances, large increases in X-rays, etc.). Predictions are generally compiled at special Regional Warning Centers, which monitor changes in the solar-terrestrial environment with satellite and ground-based instruments. Forecasters at such centers analyze these data and disperse the resulting information to their customers throughout the world.

Unfortunately, information about coronal mass ejections can't always be obtained on the timely basis required for a rapid prediction. Therefore in many situations forecasters must look for more visible signs of magnetic instabilities on the Sun (such as flares and disappearing filaments) and base their predictions on events that may actually be secondary to the true source of the storm. Adding to the difficulty, those CMEs that would affect the terrestrial environment most dramatically—events that erupt while facing toward the terrestrial neighborhood—are difficult to measure from locations near the Earth. In fact, it has been suggested that at some

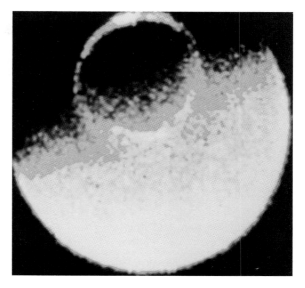

This is the first picture of the entire auroral oval taken from high latitude, and also one of the first global images received for processing at the University of Iowa from the Dynamics Explorer spacecraft. The photograph was taken September 15, 1981, from approximately 22,000 kilometers above the North Pole. The wavelengths for this image correspond to those of atomic oxygen. High intensities appear as white areas, while lesser intensities are orange. Note that the auroral oval extends across the terminator into the sunlit hemisphere of the Earth. *Photograph courtesy of NASA.*

future time CMEs be monitored by spacecraft stationed at the L4 and L5 Langrangian points (points of stability in the orbital plane of an astronomical body), where the view will be unobstructed by the Sun's glare.

In the path of magnetic storms

Large geomagnetic storms can occur any time but are about twice as likely to be felt around the equinoxes when the Earth is in a better position to receive the Sun's emissions. Overall, the number of stronger storms typically peaks twice: first, within a year or two of sunspot maximum (there is some tendency for the amplitude of this peak to correlate with the amplitude of the solar cycle), and second, several years after sunspot maximum—the so-called precursor peak. The dramatic effects of the second most severe geomagnetic storm since 1932 were felt across eastern Canada a few years ago.

March 13, 1989, dawned like any other day in Quebec, but quite suddenly strange things began to occur. Television reception faded and blurred, remote control garage doors opened and closed on their own, and then finally, for

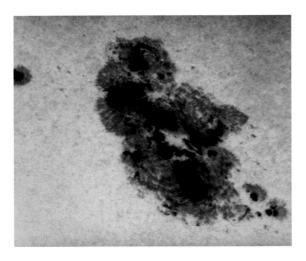

NOAA/USAF Region 5395, the huge sunspot group which spawned the great flares of March 1989, is shown in this photograph from the Sacramento Peak Observatory.

6 million Canadians, the lights went out.

Most did not realize that several days previously the Sun had begun to eject shock waves and great clouds of energetic particles into space. It emitted a series of powerful blasts, one of which became the largest solar flare to be recorded in almost 30 years. For days afterward the magnetosphere was bombarded by solar emissions traveling millions of miles per hour. The magnetosphere was buffeted by shockwaves until its normal sunward distance was compressed to within just a few Earth radii. The Earth's cage was rattled as seldom before.

Today astronomers cite such great solar storms with the same reverence early pioneers reserved for the severe blizzards of 1886. The effects were everywhere. Damage to the Quebec power system alone ran into the millions of dollars. Elsewhere the same geomagnetic storm severely damaged two of three transformers at the Salem 1 Nuclear Power Plant in New Jersey. In Texas magnetic surveys went haywire for days following the eruptions, as the Sun put on a show to remember. Aurorae, usually confined to middle and higher latitudes, turned the sky red and green with vivid all-sky displays that could be seen as far south as the Bahamas and Cuba.

About 10 percent of the manmade objects in space were temporarily lost as a direct result of this activity. Low-altitude high-inclination satellites experienced periods of uncontrolled tumbling as they transited regions of high gradients from field-aligned currents feeding auroral circuits. During one large series of solar emissions, satellite operators reported they were not aware of any satellite anomalies because their communications links to the satellites were out of operation. Several homing-pigeon racers reportedly lost nearly all their birds when the birds apparently became confused as the storms disrupted their navigation systems.

Obviously not all consequences of the Sun's outbursts are as benign as aurorae! When electrical currents of sufficient energy flow in the atmosphere their charge can be transferred into long electrical and telephone lines. More importantly, power systems have grown more vulnerable because of longer lines and larger, more efficient transformers added over the past three decades. Many of the older power systems are also susceptible and may experience strong surges and burnouts, as experienced during the 1989 storms. Even long pipelines are corroded by the chemical processes caused by these events.

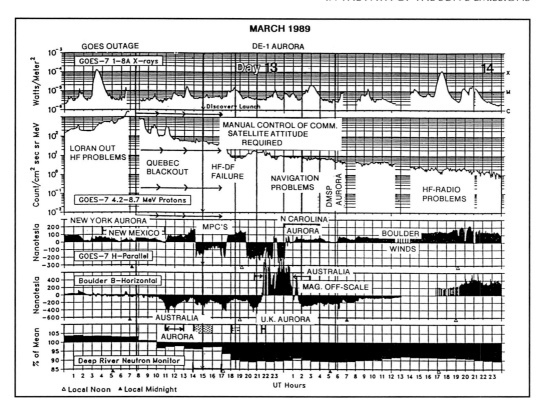

Figure 7.2. GOES-7 Solar-terrestrial environment plot for March 13/14, 1989. This busy graph shows many of the terrestrial impacts of this disturbed interval. *Diagram courtesy of National Geophysical Data Center.*

The disruption of radio and other communications facilities is yet another consequence of intense magnetic storms. The more severe difficulties begin soon after the initial outburst. Special X-ray sensors and other instruments aboard satellites are usually the first to detect these conditions. Since a portion of this radiation travels at nearly the speed of light, it begins to affect the ionosphere almost immediately after the eruption.

The ionosphere is a region of the atmosphere composed of particles (ions) that have been stripped of electrons by solar irradiation. It has the property of reflecting high-frequency radio waves, making long-distance communication possible. While radiation from the Sun interacts with components in the atmosphere to create and maintain the ionosphere, especially strong energy surges (X-rays) can cause shortwave fadeouts and other disruptions, which eventually result in a total radio blackout.

When the effects of a torrent of solar activity penetrate deep into the atmosphere and strong currents flow throughout the ionosphere, its ability to reflect radio

111

signals is changed. Signals at some frequencies are intensified and propagate, or spread, over unusually long distances (a positive effect), while others are absorbed and lose energy, resulting in a weakening or loss of the signal. Occasionally the effect is so intense that high-frequency radio communication becomes impossible. As you would expect, conditions at the poles are usually more severe than at lower latitudes. Such disruptions, known as polar cap absorptions (PCAs), result from the enhanced ionization caused by a high flux of energetic solar protons. PCAs can interfere with transpolar radio paths for days and in some cases, weeks.

Sometimes recurrent geomagnetic storms (that is, those caused by persistent coronal holes) result in an increase of energetic electrons (typically, particles with energies greater than 2 million electron-volts) in the outer magnetosphere. When these enhancements are observed in connection with geomagnetic disturbances they usually begin about a day after the onset of the storm and continue for a few days after it subsides. Significant numbers of these particles can penetrate the skin of a spacecraft and build up an electrical charge in various components. This condition is known as deep dielectric charging.

Just such a situation is illustrated by the failure of the Canadian communications satellite Anik E2, and by a number of other satellite anomalies at geosynchronous altitude during the beginning of 1994. (Geosynchronous orbit is an eastward orbit whose period is 24 hours. A satellite in such an orbit remains above the same spot on the Earth's surface.) Satellites can slowly discharge such currents, but damage to delicate electronics can occur if energy is deposited at a rate faster than it escapes, a probable occurrence when the electron flux remains high for a number of days, as it did in the case of the Anik failure.

In addition to these effects, if a single energetic particle (such as a cosmic ray or solar proton) penetrates a satellite's computer memory-circuit, the computer can reset or issue false commands that result in an invalid course and position—or even fail outright. This can be a serious problem with navigational satellites, since ships far out at sea rely on these instruments to determine their exact location.

Normally the harmful properties of solar radiation are not a severe problem for low-orbit spacecraft such as the space shuttle, since these vehicles operate at an altitude near enough to the Earth that they are safeguarded by the atmosphere. However, during the great storms that occurred in the fall of 1989, astronauts aboard the shuttle Atlantis reported irritating "flashes" in their eyes as energetic protons penetrated their optic nerves. The astronauts retreated to the most protected part of the shuttle, but the eye flashes continued until the solar proton events ended.

The Sun's powerful emissions can affect spacecraft indirectly as well as directly. A significant increase in certain radiation causes the Earth's exosphere—the portion of the upper atmosphere extending upward of 500 to 600 kilometers—to expand, which means the satellite must make its way through more atmosphere than anticipated.

Such circumstances occurred during the great storms of 1989. The exospheric temperature rose, the atmosphere expanded, and the Solar Maximum Mission satellite responded with a drop in altitude of nearly a kilometer. When no measures were taken to rescue this highly productive instrument, it went on to a flaming demise later that year.

Previously, in 1979, an exospheric expansion also related to the effects of an un-expectedly strong surge of solar activity caused the 85-ton Skylab spacecraft to disintegrate over Australia in a final blazing dive toward the Earth. Currently the only practical solution to such problems is to move the vehicle higher to a thinner but less protected part of the atmosphere, or to bring the more important instru-ments back to Earth with the shuttle.

All satellites in Earth orbit are subject to various influences that can alter their orbit. Satellites in low Earth orbit with perigee altitudes below 2000 kilometers are predominately subject to atmospheric drag. This force very slowly tends to circu-larize and reduce the altitude of the orbit. The rate of decay becomes very rapid at altitudes less than 200 kilometers, and by the time the satellite is down to 180 kilo-meters it has only a few hours to live before it makes a fiery reentry. Temperatures attained during this reentry are usually great enough to vaporize most of the satellite, but under certain conditions component pieces may reach the ground.

The rate at which a low orbit satellite orbit decays is a function of atmospheric density at each point along the orbit together with the satellite's cross-sectional area and mass. The air density varies along the orbit, as a function of latitude and longitude, time of day, time of year, and season. However, at a fixed point in space, if we average the short time variations, we find the atmospheric density can be expressed in terms of two space environment parameters. They are the solar 10-centimeter radio flux and the planetary geomagnetic index, Ap, both of which vary in concert with the sunspot cycle. As each of these increases we find a corresponding increase in atmospheric density at altitudes above 120 kilometers. The radio flux mainly determines the drag, especially since it acts for an extended period, not just on disturbed days.

The uncertainty in predicting the space environment coupled with unresolved variations in atmospheric density preclude scientists from being able to specify exactly when a satellite will reenter the atmosphere. Even sophisticated com-puter programs can only claim a prediction accuracy of about 10 percent. This means that one day before a particular reentry is due, the uncertainty in time of fall will be at least two hours. The satellite will have circled the globe within this time span.

According to National Geophysical Data Center director, J. H. Allen, the prolif-eration over the last few decades of technological systems sensitive to radiation, current, and magnetic fields; the complex maze of interlocking components such as that represented by the national electrical power grid; and the increasing pres-ence of humans in space combine to make society ever more vulnerable to distur-bances in the solar-terrestrial regime.

Moreover the apparent growth in activity on the Sun as measured at Earth by magnetic storms (at a 30-year high during the maximum of cycle 22), may com-bine with a decreasing main geomagnetic field to contribute even more to the impact of such events. To the extent that satellites in orbit, ground-based electrical generating stations, and power distribution networks are adversely affected by

113

magnetic storms—and given that their problems may be cumulative—the prospect of greater activity in the years just ahead may be significant.

Solar cycles and the climate

Do changes in the Sun's output influence our weather and climate? Good question! Weather patterns could be influenced by small changes in electrical heating in the upper atmosphere. However, nearly all proposed relationships between solar activity and the Earth's climate are highly speculative and most have been disproved over time. The apparent lack of a physical mechanism that could account for such changes is even more troubling. Solar effects by themselves are generally thought to be too weak, compared with traditional weather patterns, to produce the changes frequently attributed to them.

Perhaps the most outstanding example of a clear-cut relationship between solar activity and terrestrial weather is the drop in temperature—approximately one degree on the average—that accompanied the long period of exceptionally low solar activity known as the Maunder Minimum. During this lull many parts of Europe suffered through extremely cold weather, so cold that the interval has been referred to as a "little ice age." While a change of only a single degree seems almost insignificant, the temperature decrease was maintained over many years. The combination of time and lessened solar energy output continues to be the most likely source of these conditions.

More recent research points to a second possible connection between solar activity and the Earth's weather. Every two or three years the winds in the lower stratosphere reverse their east-to-west direction, an effect known as the quasi-biennial-oscillation, or QBO. Some studies show an association between the Sun's output of radio waves (which parallels the sunspot cycle) and the westerly phase of the QBO.

No relationship appears when the radio flux rate is compared with all stratospheric temperatures, but a striking agreement emerges when temperatures associated with the easterly wind flows are removed from consideration. Again however, no one thus far has been able to describe a mechanism that could account for this effect, posing serious problems for its acceptance. In spite of this difficulty the apparent correlation between these indices is one of the strongest ever proposed.

A different kind of influence on the Earth's climate appeared in the early 1980s, indicated by an analysis of sedimentary samples taken from ancient glacial lakes in Southern Australia and other locations. These deposits probably originated nearly 700 million years ago when they were formed by water from melting glaciers. The varying thickness of the annual deposits, known as varves, was first thought to result from changes in temperature related to the Sun's activity. Samples seemed to show the 11-year sunspot cycle and the 22-year magnetic cycle also appeared.

As convincing as such records appeared, at least one new investigation has concluded that varves might not be related to solar activity at all. Instead, the pattern may be the result of a cycle of spring and neap tides.

A comparable relationship expressed in ancient tree rings was investigated by A. E. Douglas in Arizona more than a half century ago. Interestingly, the branch of scientific study that Douglas founded, dendochronology, has been used to explain the disappearance of the Anasazi Indians, whom we met earlier. Douglas believed the very narrow tree rings he encountered indicated a prolonged drought between 1276 and 1299—the same time the tribes of the Four Corners region vanished. His research also seemed to show a relationship between annual ring thickness and sunspot cycle, the thicker rings indicating increased growth due to warmer growing seasons. However, similar examples show no correlation, and Douglas' findings could have resulted from chance occurrences.

On the other hand, a modern study of 2000-year-old pine trees high on the Sierra Nevada in the southwestern United States appears to show a correlation between the production of carbon 14, a component of the Earth's atmosphere, and tree ring growth. This research shows that in the past large changes occurred in both simultaneously, and that one coincided with the Maunder Minimum. If this new finding is eventually borne out, the role we believe the Sun plays in global warming could be increased.

When evaluating long-term trends such as global warming, we should keep several things in mind: The instruments for measuring these changes have not been in use for very long—the thermometer itself has only existed for a few hundred years—there has been no significant change in summer temperatures for nearly 130 years, and the frightening computer-based forecasts of the 1980s have not come to pass. While it is prudent to take the initial steps to avoid such an event before it takes place, we should remember that at present the situation remains unclear.

In any event, a direct causal relationship between solar activity and terrestrial weather must be tenuous at best since the effect itself would be comparatively small. We may eventually learn that solar activity simply triggers a more powerful series of events, or that even very small effects produce changes which are somehow magnified beyond current expectations. At this time, however, a physical mechanism that could produce a noticeable difference in Earth's climate still eludes us.

Where do we go from here? The space project International Solar Terrestrial Physics Mission (ISTP) will try to solve many of the remaining questions relating to the energy flow between Sun and Earth. The aim of the ISTP program is to understand the physics of the Sun-Earth relationship in order to predict how the Earth's atmosphere will respond to changes in the solar wind. This multinational effort involves scientists and equipment from the United States, Europe, Russia, and Japan. Perhaps as the data from the Wind and Polar spacecraft are evaluated, the long-sought precise link between solar and terrestrial activity—one of the oldest mysteries in geomagnetism—will be found.

A Simple Magnetometer

Several years ago, R. J. Livesey, the director of the Aurora Section of the British Astronomical Association, devised a neat little device he calls the "jam-jar" magnetometer. (Livesey's apparatus was described in the October 1989 issue of *Sky & Telescope* magazine.) The instrument is designed to detect fluctuations in the Earth's magnetic field, and is based on magnetometer principles developed by Gauss and his collaborators during the 19th century. Since such variations serve to indicate increased solar activity, the device can be used as a detector of aurorae.

Livesey (see appendix for address) normally reads his magnetometer about once an hour. When activity rises he makes his observations more frequently, and if a major geomagnetic storm occurs he monitors it almost continuously. Although more elaborate devices can be constructed, this is an inexpensive and easily built version; it's sure to boost your reputation as an aurora forecaster!

Materials:

• A wide-mouth glass jar about 8 cm in diameter and 18 cm high, with a plastic screw-on lid (we used a mustard jar)
• A 20-cm length of thin nylon thread
• Small bar magnet about 2 cm long

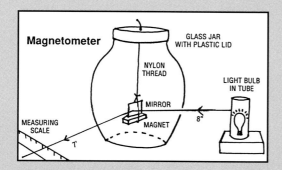

• Small first-surface mirror about 1/2 by 1 cm high (A first-surface mirror is silvered on its face, rather than back.)
• A clear 6-volt DC light bulb, a matching bulb socket and small 6-volt battery to power the bulb
• A short section of thin-walled tubing (to enclose the bulb)
• Construction paper, epoxy glue, small amount of dull black paint
• Scrap piece of wood to be used as a base for the bulb unit
• Length of insulated single strand copper wire
• A strip of white cardboard that can be used as an optical movement scale

Construction:

Paint the mirror face dull black, leaving a thin vertical strip in its center, approximately 1 mm wide.

Refer to the illustrations during the following steps:

Glue the mirror to the top of the magnet.

Strip a short section of the wire and construct a sling to hold the magnet and mirror.

Drill a small hole in the center of the lid. Glue the nylon thread to the sling and suspend the mirror-magnet by pulling the thread through the hole. Screw the lid to the jar and adjust the thread's length so the magnet hangs just a bit above the bottom of the jar. Secure the thread. (If the magnet swings too easily you may need to glue small pieces of construction paper to the sides and back of the magnet, which will reduce its tendency to swing. Don't block the thin strip of mirror.).

Cut a thin vertical slot in the short (3- to 4-cm) section of the tubing that will enclose the bulb. The sides of the slot must be smooth and straight; if this proves difficult,

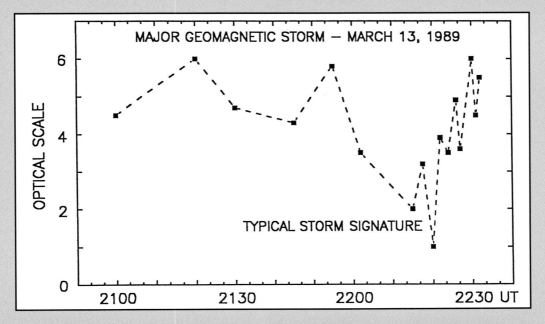

Figure 1. R. J. Livesey recorded these geomagnetic effects during one of the great solar storms that occurred in March 1989.

use a razor blade on either side of the opening to achieve the desired effect. Attach the bulb socket to the wood base. Place the bulb into the socket, which should be connected to the battery with short pieces of insulated wire. Place the tubing over the bulb assembly, locating the bulb just behind the slit, forming the light source.

Scale the strip of white cardboard by marking, and numbering consecutively, equally spaced steps along the horizontal axis of the strip.

Procedure:

For the magnetometer site, choose a dimly lit room located as far as possible from heavy metal objects (especially cars) and as free as possible from electrical appliances. Arrange the device as illustrated, and allow the magnet to come to a rest. The lamp should be placed 20 to 40 cm from the jar, with the scale at the same height but about 2 meters away.

To take a magnetic observation, stand facing the jar, and while moving your head from right to left note where the light beam reflected onto the scale appears brightest. Record the date, time, and scale reading. Do not try to compare measurements directly from day to day, since local conditions can affect such readings (Figure 1). Rather, try to compile a group of measurements during a single magnetic storm that indicate changes in the series of readings. These data can then be plotted according to time, demonstrating the character of the disturbance.

According to Livesey, when a magnetic storm is in progress readings will fluctuate considerably, and you should take measurements as frequently as possible. If the magnetometer is very active, look for aurorae that evening, particularly if you live above about 40 degrees latitude. Do you detect more or less geomagnetic activity during the March and September equinoxes?

117

8
Solar Eclipses

It is difficult to imagine the terror our earliest ancestors must have felt when, suddenly and without warning at midday, the temperature plummeted, darkness fell, and the Sun disappeared. Perhaps they feared a monster had devoured the Sun or that the gods were punishing them. We have no written records from Neolithic peoples, but we can gain some insight through the many exotic myths of more recent cultures that sought to interpret eclipses.

The Hindu legend of Rahu provides a typical example. In this tale a poor man named Rahu offended the gods by drinking a sacred liquid. In retaliation the gods struck off Rahu's head and placed it high in the sky as a planet. According to the legend the severed head of Rahu continues to chase the Sun and Moon throughout eternity, occasionally swallowing one or the other and causing an eclipse.

In other primitive tales, the Sun—often regarded as a person by the ancients—sometimes vanishes for an appropriate period of time because of "his" displeasure with the wickedness of humanity. Or alternatively the Sun may be carried off and imprisoned, requiring a superhuman effort by some mythical person or beast to ensure its return. Such drastic situations usually can only be resolved through unbridled repentance, sacrifice, and prayer.

Throughout the ancient Orient eclipses were thought to result from a leader's actions and were regarded as important omens. The book *History of the Former Han Dynasty* relates the warning words of one Chinese ruler: "When the prince of men is not virtuous, a reproach appears in heaven and earth. . . . Our experience in governing has been only for a brief time, so that we must not have been correct in our acts; hence during wu-shen there was an eclipse of the Sun and an earthquake. We are greatly dismayed!"

As we might expect, the drama accompanying an unexpected eclipse of the Sun virtually assured that the events would be recorded. In Chapter One we mentioned that the oldest account of an eclipse was probably recorded during the Chinese Hsia Dynasty (2183 to 1751 B.C.). Several centuries later (1375 B.C.) the Syrians described an event that appears to have been a solar eclipse, and historians believe the Chinese also recorded eclipses through inscriptions on oracle bones dating from about 1700 to 1100 B.C.

Unfortunately, many of these accounts speak of the Sun and eclipses only obliquely, and so some researchers doubt their authenticity as eclipse records. However, a specific reference to at least one eclipse does appear in the ancient Assyrian chronicles. The description unequivocally points to an eclipse that occurred in 763 B.C.: "Insurrection in the city of Assur. In the month of Sivan, the Sun was eclipsed." Like many of their contemporaries, the Assyrians believed events on Earth were initiated by phenomena in a spirit-filled sky (not too far from the mark!), and therefore that eclipses were significant events.

To the ancients an unanticipated solar eclipse was mystifying and because their cause was generally unknown, terrifying as well. Around 585 B.C., the Greek historian Herodotus wrote of a battle between the Medes and the Lydians that ended when the frightened soldiers fled during an eclipse. The account goes on to state that the sudden onset of darkness so startled the Medes and Lydians that they abandoned their five-year war and sealed the peace with a double marriage.

Even later, in parts of the world where they were better understood, eclipses were often seen as portents of doom. According to an early entry in the *Anglo-Saxon Chronicles*: "In this year King Henry went overseas at Lammas, and the next day, when he was lying asleep on board ship, the day grew dark

The annular eclipse of January 4, 1992, in a ring of setting sunlight over the Pacific Ocean off the San Diego coast at Crystal Pier, California. During an annular eclipse the Moon is too far from the Earth to entirely obscure the Sun and produces a dramatic "ring of fire." *The photograph was taken by W. Livingston of the National Solar Observatory, Kitt Peak (NOAO).*

over all lands, and the Sun became as if it were a three-night's-old Moon, with stars about it at midday. People were very much astonished and terrified, and said that something important would be bound to come after this—and so it did, for during that same year the King died. . . ."

All well and good, but another factor plays a part in some of these accounts. Early historians, astrologers, and monks were often more influenced by the needs of the royal family or State than the requirements of accuracy. They were occasionally disposed to manipulate, or in some cases invent, the dates of dramatic events like eclipses and use them for their own purposes.

We can see an example of this in the linking of a solar eclipse with the death of King Henry. It is virtually certain that Henry died in A.D. 1135; but the solar eclipse that was credited with predicting his demise actually occurred two years earlier. Nonetheless the association of a king's death with an eclipse of the Sun demonstrates the powerful influence such events held.

Although they were frightened by eclipses, our forebears tried their best to understand them. Like many superstitious people, they apparently believed that if eclipses could be foretold an act of good will could be offered to the spirits before the event that might somehow hold the eclipse at bay. Unfortunately, such beliefs initiated many questionable predictions.

In early Japan, for instance, fewer than 20 percent of solar eclipses predicted to occur before A.D. 1600 were actually observed. Why? Because if a forecast eclipse did not take place, its absence was credited to the ruler's high virtue or intervention. As a result, royal power was enhanced, and the court astrologer was frequently rewarded. On the other hand, if a solar eclipse occurred that had not been foreseen, there was no time to ward off danger, and the court astrologer might very well face execution. As you can see, it was far better for the astrologer to predict as many eclipses as possible and hope for the best.

Sadly, the fear generated by an eclipse is not confined to the ancients. As recently as 1914 Russian peasants fled to their churches in horror and despair after a total solar eclipse occurred in the Ukraine. And at the 1922 Australian eclipse, aborigines believed the astronomers who had gathered at a nearby site to view the event were trying to capture the Sun in a net. Even today, primitive people in some remote parts of the world continue to fear eclipses. At the November 1994 eclipse Indians high in the Andean Mountains lit fires to keep the Earth warm during totality. An even more complex ritual is employed by the Ata Manobo of Davao del Norte in the Philippines, who link eclipses to legends of diabolical monsters in the sky.

The Ata Manobo believe a giant snake swallows the Sun (or Moon, during a lunar eclipse) and then descends to Earth to do the same to mankind. When an eclipse occurs the Ata Manobo beat tin cans, kettles, and plates while shouting in loud voices "luwo!" (throw-off!) in an effort to make the monster spew out the Sun. Hopefully the 15,000 Ata Manobo and others in similar circumstances will sooner or later receive an education that will allow them to enjoy these events with the same enthusiasm as the rest of us.

Early scientific investigations

Not all our early predecessors were frozen with fear and superstition during an eclipse. In particular, ancient Greek scholars viewed such things with scientific interest. One of the earliest experiments to use an eclipse as an investigative tool was carried out by the great Greek astronomer Hipparchus in 130 B.C., as he sought to determine the diameters and distances of the Sun and Moon.

Hipparchus understood the true nature of eclipses, realized the Earth was a sphere, and knew the Earth's approximate diameter. During a lunar eclipse he used measurements of the Earth's curved shadow to determine the shadow's diameter at the distance of the Moon. He then prepared a scale diagram that showed these data along with the angle subtended by the Sun. The method was sound but limited by the extremely tiny angles produced by the enormous difference in distance between the Moon and Sun. Apparently Hipparchus realized this weakness and redetermined the Moon's distance, arriving at a result of 62 to 74

Earth radii. Not bad when compared with a modern value of a bit over 60 radii!

Unfortunately, Hipparchus then employed Aristarchus' estimate, which set a lower limit on the Sun's distance from the Earth of about 19 times that of the Moon. Aristarchus may have been the first to recognize that the Earth and planets orbited the Sun, but his estimate of this ratio was far too low. Therefore, Hipparchus' calculations of the solar diameter and distance using this value were also much too small. These measurements were the best by ancient astronomers, however, and remained substantially unchallenged until the 17th century.

When they can be adequately verified, eclipses are a valuable tool for historians, since an accurate eclipse account establishes a precise date in the past. One of the more extensive compilations of such information is represented by Ptolemy's great work Almagest (A.D. 140), one of a surprisingly small number of early European records. The work includes a list of the kings of ancient Babylon, Assyria, and Persia that can be linked with the eclipse record, in some cases firmly fixing the dates of eastern chronology.

The high regard with which knowledge of eclipses and other astronomical phenomena was held in the early Orient is amply demonstrated by a letter written by Francis Xavier, a Jesuit priest who helped bring Christianity to Japan. In his letters Xavier stated that any priests coming to Japan would be "at an advantage if they were well acquainted with cosmic phenomena because the Japanese are enthusiastic about listening to explanations of planetary motion and solar eclipses." Xavier even reported instances of Japanese citizens who converted to Christianity because of the supposed superiority of western astronomy.

Judging from the written record, learned men have tried to forecast eclipses throughout history. Earlier we discussed Thales and the possibility that he predicted the eclipse that stopped a battle between the Medes and Lydians. But long before that time the early Babylonians began to compile the eclipse annals that eventually made Thales' forecast feasible. Moreover, by this time the ancient Greeks and Chaldeans, in contrast to their contemporaries, had conceived of eclipses as cyclical. And one or the other—most likely the Greeks—went on to uncover the important concept of the saros (see below).

In spite of such long-held interest, eclipses have played a vital role in the scientific understanding of the Sun only since the early 17th century and more especially since the mid-19th century. During these periods of great scientific enlightenment, but before the invention of the coronagraph and other modern instruments, they offered astronomers an opportunity to observe the prominences, corona, and chromosphere—features which were totally invisible at other times.

How eclipses occur

From the record we know that around 35 percent of all eclipses are partial no matter the location of the observer, 32 percent are annular, and 28 percent are total somewhere on the Earth. The small remainder consists of special combinations of annular and total. Normally we need not concern ourselves with these few, since they occur only rarely. They take place under very special circumstances, such as an unusual separation between the Earth and Moon, or when

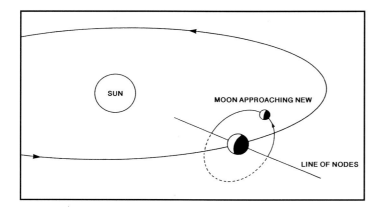

Figure 8.1. The Moon's orbit intersects the ecliptic (the great circle made by the intersection of the plane of the Earth's orbit with the celestial sphere) at two places called nodes. A line extending through these points—the line of nodes—must point directly at the Sun for an eclipse to occur.

the lunar shadow contacts the Earth at an odd angle.

If the Moon's orbit were in the same plane as the Earth's (the ecliptic), an eclipse could take place every month at New Moon. However, its path is inclined from the ecliptic by about 5 degrees. The orbital planes of the Earth and Moon intersect twice each month at places called nodes. When an imaginary line extending through these points (the line of nodes) is aimed directly at the Sun, a total solar eclipse can occur.

For this to take place, however, several additional requirements must be met. The Moon's orbit is not circular but elliptical. Therefore, the Moon must be at a distance near enough to the Earth that its dark central shadow, the umbral shadow, touches the Earth's surface. If it does not, but all other conditions are fulfilled, an annular eclipse occurs. Alternatively, an observer located within the Moon's outer, or penumbral, shadow sees only a partial eclipse. Interestingly, the remaining sunlight during partial eclipses is often so intense that many are totally unaware anything out of the ordinary is happening.

Only when the Moon's apparent diameter is large enough to completely block the Sun—that is, when the nearly new Moon is near its closest approach to the Earth—can a total eclipse occur. Then a fortuitous natural circumstance comes into play, one which deals with the relative diameters of Sun and Moon. The Moon is approximately 1/400 the Sun's diameter, but also lies about 400 times closer to the Earth. Were it not for this unique situation, we could never witness a total eclipse.

All these conditions can occur simultaneously only when the Sun is at opposite locations on the celestial sphere. Consequently, there is an eclipse season that repeats at intervals of about six months. There is, however, some latitude in the relative positions of Sun, Earth, and Moon that will still allow an eclipse to occur; so more than two solar eclipses are possible during a single year.

It may seem surprising in view of the notoriety associated with many solar eclipses, but during many years more eclipses of the Sun can take place than those of the Moon. The greatest number of solar eclipses that can take place in any one year is five, but this is a rare occurrence. (When the geometry is just right, two eclipses can take place near each node. And in the event 13 new moons occur in a single year, a fifth eclipse is also possible.) Two, three, and four eclipses can also occur during a single year. On the average, a total solar eclipse takes place only once in each 1½ years.

The saros

To nicely complicate the situation, the plane of the Moon's orbit does not remain at the same position on the ecliptic plane but gradually shifts its location westward, completing the rotation in slightly over 18½ years. Since the nodes regress along the orbital path, the Sun crosses the same node of the Moon's orbit in a little less than one year (346.62 days). This interval is called the eclipse year, and is believed to have first been identified by Chaldean astronomers around 300 B.C. The discovery of the eclipse year is almost certainly rooted in the study of eclipses begun by the Babylonians. Eventually a pattern emerged from these records. Eclipses repeated themselves in a little over 18 years (18 years, plus either 10⅓ or 11⅓ days, depending on the number of intervening leap years). The unearthing of such cycles, known as the saros (from the Greek word for repetition) is often credited to the Babylonians. However, the preponderance of evidence now seems to favor the ancient Greeks for the actual discovery of this cycle.

A little simple mathematics demonstrates the importance of the saros and helps us to understand its use in the forecasting of eclipses. The synodic month (the period between successive New Moons) is about 29.53 days. Therefore, in yet another remarkable coincidence, the lengths (in days) of 223 lunar cycles and 19 eclipse years are very nearly identical. This circumstance causes eclipses that are close duplicates to occur after intervals of about 18 years.

Consecutive eclipses within a given saros series are similar in type and duration because the Sun and Moon have then returned to near their original positions. But they do not take place at the same location because there is a difference

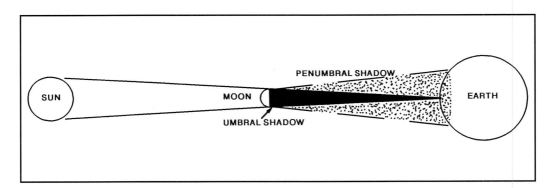

Figure 8.2. The Moon's shadow is composed of two parts: the dark umbral shadow and the outer penumbral shadow. Observers stationed within the path of the umbral shadow observe a total eclipse, while those within the penumbral shadow see only a partial eclipse. The Moon is farther away from the Earth during an annular eclipse. Thus its shadow does not reach the Earth's surface and those located within the central eclipse path see a ring of solar photosphere which appears to surround the Moon.

of ⅓ day between the lengths of 223 lunar cycles and 19 eclipse years. This factor allows the Earth to rotate through an additional 120 degrees of longitude and causes the forthcoming eclipse to fall to the west of the earlier event. During the length of a single saros an average of 42 eclipses occur, all but one related to additional Saros series. Incredible as it seems, this means that 42 separate series are operating at the same time.

Now bear with all this just a bit longer. On average, a saros cycle contains 73 eclipses and lasts for approximately 1315 years. Every series begins with an eclipse at high latitude in either the Northern or Southern Hemisphere, depending upon whether the Moon is crossing the ascending or descending orbital node. Then for a time succeeding eclipses gradually take place closer and closer to the equator. (There can be brief excursions from this routine, primarily when the Earth passes through the vernal equinox and the eclipse path is shifted for a few events.) The series begins with a group of partial eclipses that change to annular or total as the winding eclipse path approaches mid-latitudes. The saros then continues moving toward the opposite pole and the eclipse types slowly reverse. The group of cycles ends as a last partial eclipse occurs near the pole.

To illustrate the development of a series, here is a description of Saros 133, which originally appeared in NASA Reference Publication 1318. The total eclipse that began in South America and ended off the coast of South Africa in November 1994 was a member of Saros 133.

The November eclipse was the 44th member of Saros 133. The series began in A.D. 1219 with a partial eclipse in the Northern Hemisphere. During the next two centuries a dozen partial eclipses occurred, with the eclipse magnitude of each succeeding event gradually increasing. Finally, the first central eclipse—an annular eclipse—occurred in 1435. (A central eclipse is a total or annular eclipse.) The five following eclipses were also annular, with decreasing umbral durations.

The 19th event occurred in 1544 and was annular-total in nature. From the mid-16th through mid-19th centuries, the series continued to produce total eclipses with increasing durations. The trend culminated in a total eclipse in 1850 with a duration of nearly seven minutes that passed through the Hawaiian Islands.

Saros 133 continued to produce total eclipses throughout the 20th century, but their duration has regularly decreased. During the next 150 years each successive eclipse path will move deeper into the Southern Hemisphere, and their duration will gradually diminish. The final total eclipse will occur in 2373, and thereafter the remaining eclipses will be partial. The final eclipse in Saros 133—number 72 in this series—will be a partial eclipse in the far Southern Hemisphere in 2499.

Eclipse observation

The path of a total eclipse is fairly narrow, less than a little over 250 kilometers across, because the Moon's orbit never allows a very wide umbral shadow. The typical eclipse path, however, is only about 160 kilometers wide and perhaps 9500 kilometers long. For this and other reasons, the probability that an eclipse will recur at any one place in the world is only about once every 450 years, so those who wish to see a total eclipse must almost always travel long distances.

Here we see the solar corona during a total solar eclipse. Several solar prominences can be seen as pinkish features near the edge of the Moon. Surrounding these prominences is the hot coronal gas, which in this case appears to be white and diffuse. The interaction between the relatively cool prominence gas and the hot coronal gas is a topic of current research. *Photograph courtesy of National Solar Observatory/Sacramento Peak.*

When viewing a partial or annular eclipse, or the partial phases of a total eclipse, some proven technique that protects the observer's eyesight is mandatory. The same precautions that apply to viewing the Sun under normal, non-eclipse conditions must be followed throughout all the partial phases and for an entire annular eclipse. Such stipulations apply to both telescopic and optically un-assisted viewing.

For the latter, an unmarked square of shade 14 welder's glass offers good eye protection before and after maximum total eclipse, as well as during partial and annular events. When viewing any eclipse telescopically the observer must use normal solar filtering, as described in Chapter 10. The filter or welder's glass can only be discarded during the maximum phase of a total eclipse, which begins as the last glimmer of sunlight disappears behind the advancing Moon. At the end of totality, when the first tiny bits of sunlight appear along the Moon's trailing limb, the observer must immediately reemploy these devices.

As we watch an eclipse unfold it is useful to divide the event into four specific developmental stages, or contacts. (The Alexandrian astronomer Theon is likely to have been the first to make similar measurements during the eclipse of A.D. 365, using a water clock to record the beginning, maximum, and end of that eclipse.) For observers in the Northern Hemisphere a typical eclipse takes place in the southern sky as the Moon overtakes the Sun from the west. The first contact is the instant of external tangency between the two bodies. It occurs at the moment the Moon's leading limb first appears to touch the Sun, and signals the onset of partial eclipse.

If the eclipse is annular more of the disk becomes obscured until second contact, when the Moon can first be seen projected against the Sun's disk in its entirety. Then an observer located near the center of the eclipse path—one standing within the extension of the Moon's shadow—sees a bright ring of sunlight surrounding the Moon, the so-called "ring of fire."

During an annular eclipse the spectacular phenomena that can be seen during a total eclipse—prominences, chromosphere, and corona—continue to be hidden by the brilliant circle of light from the remaining photosphere. On the other hand, if the Moon's apparent diameter is just a little smaller than the Sun's, an observer near the central eclipse path may see the Sun ringed by a bright "necklace" made up of beads of sunlight shining through breaks in the lunar mountains.

Darkness does not accompany annular eclipses, but a sort of eerie twilight descends and the temperature may decrease noticeably (several degrees) at eclipse maximum. Similar circumstances occur during partial eclipses after the Sun's disk is about 75 percent obscured. An extremely brief period of darkness occurs during the rare annular-total-annular eclipse; the dark central shadow of the Moon touches the Earth for only a moment, resulting in just a few seconds of totality.

In the case of a typical total eclipse, the Moon's dark shadow appears on the horizon just before the onset of eclipse maximum, looking as if it were a gigantic storm. The shadow rushes across the landscape at more than 1700 kilometers per hour. (It can travel five or more times more quickly at high latitudes.) Observers may notice rapid changes of color just before the shadow passes the twilight landscape. Suddenly the sky darkens sharply and Baily's beads appear along the advancing lunar limb as a few remaining bright points of sunlight thread their way through the Moon's rugged terrain.

After the annular eclipse of 1836, Francis Baily called attention to the bead phenomenon. However, this phenomenon had been noticed long before Baily's description, and by no less an astronomer than famed comet discoverer Edmund Halley, who mentioned the effect a century before. During the Revolutionary War members of the Harvard/American Academy of Sciences also noted the beads during their expedition to the eclipse of 1780. Another familiar eclipse feature, the diamond ring, occurs when a single brilliant ray of sunlight bursts through a deep lunar valley and outshines all others.

For those observers located somewhere near the center line of a total eclipse, second contact occurs when the beads suddenly disappear and the reddish chromosphere springs into view—the onset of totality. The glowing photosphere

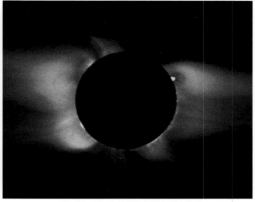

Two views of solar corona, showing differences in the Sun's atmosphere at solar cycle maximum (left, February 1980), and about 1.5 years after minimum (right, March 1988). Both of these photographs were taken with a camera developed by G. A. Newkirk, Jr. This specialized instrument photgraphs the corona in red light—6400Å—through a radially graded filter that suppresses the bright inner corona in order to show the much fainter streamers of the outer corona in the same photograph. *Photographs courtesy of the High Altitude Observatory, National Center for Atmospheric Research.*

is now completely obscured by the black lunar disk, and if any prominences are present, they too appear along the limb, stretching into space for up to tens of thousands of kilometers.

After a moment or so the Sun's gauzy, pearl-white corona—first described in the West by Kepler in 1605—becomes visible. The combination of coronal and scattered terrestrial light is about as bright as the Full Moon, so the sky generally does not become totally dark. Still, depending upon their altitude above the horizon, Capella, Procyon, Sirius, Pollux and Castor can often be seen along with at least some of the brighter planets.

The pattern of coronal streamers and coronal holes changes systematically throughout the solar activity cycle. At times of high activity, when many sunspots are visible, streamers and holes appear almost randomly around the Sun. At times of low activity, when few sunspots are present, there are large coronal holes in the polar regions of the Sun and bright streamers emanate from near the solar equator.

As you may suspect, the geometric structure is visible in the pattern of fine striations and magnetic structure of the corona, much as the magnetic field of a bar magnet can be visualized by the pattern assumed by iron filings sprinkled around it. Coronal structures reflect the magnetic geometry because protons and electrons can move freely along the lines of magnetic force, but not across them.

Central eclipse persists for a longer interval near the equator because at low latitudes the counteracting effect produced by the Earth's rotation is greatest. If we were to measure the actual speed of the lunar shadow, we would find it in excess of 3300 kilometers per hour.

However, the Earth rotates in the direction of the shadow's path, which slows the shadow's passage drastically. Even so, totality is always less than about 7

The "diamond ring" eclipse effect is caused by the Moon covering all but a tiny sliver of the Sun. This photograph was taken on February 16, 1980, by National Solar Observatory astronomers at Hyderabad, India. *Photograph courtesy of NOAO.*

minutes, 40 seconds. (The Moon's motion is faster when it is nearest Earth and slower when farthest; and the relative apparent size of solar and lunar disks also plays a part in determining the length of totality.) At higher latitudes the Earth's speed of rotation is smaller, so the shadow's speed is relatively higher and the length of totality, or centrality, correspondingly less.

Third contact occurs when the Moon's leading limb marks the instant of internal tangency with the solar disk. During a total eclipse, the corona fades from view, is replaced briefly by a reappearance of the chromosphere, and totality ends. For center line observers, Baily's beads or the diamond ring may return along the trailing limb of the Moon, but they fade rapidly. On the heels of their disappearance a gradually diminishing partial eclipse occurs until finally—and always too soon—fourth contact arrives as the Moon appears to take its last small bite from the solar disk. A marvelous spectacle.

Although eclipses no longer play the important scientific role that they once did, they will always be unforgettable for those who witness them. No other celestial display can compare with the beauty and drama of a total solar eclipse. Only then is the exquisite majesty and enormous energy of the Sun most apparent.

Capturing a Solar Eclipse on Video

You've gotten pretty good at capturing family vacations with the camcorder. Now you want to shoot footage of some of Nature's more spectacular astronomical phenomena, but you're not quite ready for CCD (electronic camera). If only you could use the equipment you already have. Well, you're in luck! Try the following simple procedure to record one of the most glorious sights imaginable—a solar eclipse.

Materials:

- A camcorder with fully charged battery, or AC adaptor
- A tripod
- A solar filter
- Videotape and an extra battery
- A solar eclipse!
  (A partial eclipse will do.)

Be sure all your equipment is working, batteries are charged, and videotape is in the camera. Sometimes it's the obvious things that slip by us. Jim Marsh of Troy, Missouri, drove to the Texas-New Mexico border to tape the May 1994 annular eclipse. Jim arrived, but Jim's film didn't. Fortunately a convenience store owner lent Jim the tape out of the store's security camera!)

Preparing for the eclipse:

You don't have to wait for an eclipse to know if your technique works. A week or so before the event set up your equipment just as you would for the eclipse, but for this test, target the Moon. The Sun's corona is about the same overall brightness as the Full Moon, and the Sun appears to have about the same angular diameter. Experiment with magnifications and any other variables that might occur during the eclipse itself. Such a test procedure will point up any problems in setup, operation, or battery life . . . in a hurry!

Next, a few days before the eclipse, set up your video equipment and filters and film the Sun. This way you can avoid filtering problems. According to Jim Marsh, a Mylar filter may cause a "flare" of its own if it is not drawn tightly across the lens. He suggests testing at around the time the eclipse will occur and again near sundown to become familiar with the varying degrees of sunlight seen during an eclipse.

On eclipse day, you'll be prepared. Generally it's good to set the camcorder to the standard maximum zoom—or you may wish to use a magnification you decided upon while testing. You might also want to add a converter lens. Remember that if you do use a converter you're adding one more piece of glass to the system, and potentially degrading the image somewhat.

An 8:1 or 10:1 zoom usually will allow enough space around the Sun to account for the corona. Before filming any of the partial phases, cover the lens with a solar filter. It can easily be removed during totality (don't forget!). Chapter 10 contains a discussion of the various filters available for optical use, and the same rules will apply for this purpose. In general, a Mylar filter will yield a bluish image (which can be partially corrected with a Kodak Wratten #21 filter), and a glass filter will produce the more familiar yellow-orange image of the Sun.

Don't be afraid to change from the highest zoom level occasionally and tape some wide-angle footage. After all, an eclipse doesn't take place in a vacuum—it's part of a grand scene. During the 1991 annular eclipse off the California coast, the Sun was at central eclipse at sunset just before it

Solar Eclipses 1996–2012

Date	Type	Duration	Ratio	Area
1997 Mar 9	T	2:50	1.042	Siberia
1998 Feb 26	T	4:08	1.044	Pacific Ocean, N of S America
1998 Aug 22	A	3:14	0.973	Sumatra, Borneo, Pacific Ocean
1999 Feb 16	A	1:19	0.993	Indian Ocean, Australia
1999 Aug 11	T	2:23	1.029	Atlantic Ocean, Europe, SE Asia
2001 Jun 21	T	4:56	1.050	Atlantic Ocean, S Africa, Madagascar
2001 Dec 14	A	3:54	0.968	Pacific Ocean, Central America
2002 Jun 10	A	1:13	0.996	Pacific Ocean
2002 Dec 4	T	2:04	1.024	S Africa, Indian Ocean, Australia
2003 May 31	A	3:37	0.938	Iceland
2003 Nov 23	T	1:57	1.038	Antarctica
2005 Apr 8	*	0:42	1.007	Pacific Ocean, Central America, N of S America
2005 Oct 3	A	4:32	0.958	Atlantic Ocean, Spain, Africa, Indian Ocean
2006 Mar 29	T	4:07	1.051	Atlantic Ocean, Africa, Turkey
2006 Sep 22	A	7:09	0.935	NE of S America, Atlantic Ocean, S Indian Ocean
2008 Feb 7	A	2:14	0.965	S Pacific Ocean, Antarctica
2008 Aug 1	T	2:28	1.039	N Canada, Arctic Ocean, Siberia, China
2009 Jan 26	A	7:56	0.928	S Atlantic Ocean, Indian Ocean, Sumatra, Borneo
2009 Jul 22	T	6:40	1.080	Asia, Pacific Ocean
2010 Jan 15	A	11:10	0.919	Africa, Indian Ocean, S/SE Asia
2010 Jul 11	T	5:20	1.058	Pacific Ocean, extreme S South America
2012 May 20	A	5:47	0.944	China, Japan, N Pacific Ocean, USA
2012 Nov 13	T	4:02	1.050	N Australia, Pacific Ocean

A—Annular eclipse.
T—Total eclipse.
*—Annular-total. The eclipse is total for part of the path, annular for the remainder.
Duration—The maximum duration of the total or annular phase on the central line of the eclipse path.
Ratio—The maximum value of the ratio of the Moon's disk to that of the Sun, at central eclipse.
(Compiled from Astronomical Tables of the Sun, Moon and Planets, Jean Meeus, 1983.)

sank below the Pacific Ocean. A friend of ours taped the event using a variety of magnifications. In replaying the film, the moments of high magnification were magnificent, but the wide-angle views were every bit as memorable. The lapping sound of the waves, the cries of the sea birds, and the exclamations of the eclipse-watchers as the clouds parted and the "ring of fire" finally appeared were captured with a far richer flavor than one consisting only of close-up views of the Sun and Moon.

You may also wish to mix footage of the Sun with close-ups of a large thermometer and clock to show temperature variations as the event progresses. And don't forget to look around for other evidence of the eclipse. During the 1994 annular eclipse Marsh and others noted that a large image of the Sun was reflected off a nearby observer's full-aperture filter and onto a parked truck. Another interesting scene occurred during the 1991 total eclipse in Mexico. During partial eclipse, sunlight flooding through palm fronds cast a myriad of tiny eclipse images onto the side of a sleeping 400-pound hog! Use your imagination, and have fun!

9
The Future

Like the ancients, we also track the Sun in its daily journey across the sky. But unlike our early ancestors we've learned that eclipses don't herald the end of the world any more than a Sun god engages in nightly battles with strange creatures from the underworld. In the few centuries since Galileo first turned his telescope toward the sky our scientific knowledge has leaped forward at an astonishing pace. But a number of fundamental questions about the Sun remain to be solved. The mechanism that heats the corona to its extraordinary temperature, the true nature of the solar dynamo or other source of the various active phenomena we monitor so faithfully, the Sun's interior structure and characteristics, and the "missing" neutrino problem all continue to puzzle scientists.

For the foreseeable future, experiments such as Flare Genesis will continue to play a prominent role in the search for answers. Instruments on space vehicles are wondrous technological achievements, but the projects are expensive, not really suited to long observational runs, and not nearly as adaptable to change as those on Earth or carried aloft by balloon. On the other hand, precise observations of some solar phenomena can only be obtained from space, so future research must encompass all avenues of observational astronomy.

Despite its relatively high cost the U.S. space science program

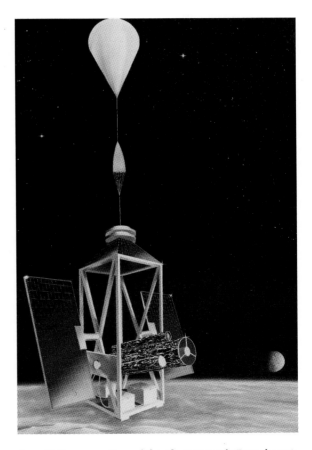

An artist's conception of the Flare Genesis Experiment floating over Antarctica. The height of the gondola will be ≈ 5 meters. The main telescope has an 80-centimeter aperture and a 5-arc-minute field of view. The target selector telescope has a 10-centimeter aperture and a 1-degree field of view. *Photograph courtesy of D. Rust, Applied Physics Laboratory, Johns Hopkins University.*

has been enormously productive. Now the first steps have been taken toward shaping the space science programs of the 21st century. It will be challenging and very different from what might have been envisioned only a short time ago, but the program will undoubtedly remain in the forefront of science, technology, and education.

We are often asked if solar activity indices such as Wolf's long-running series of relative sunspot numbers will endure. In the immediate future—for the next several decades at least, and perhaps well beyond—we believe it is very likely. New techniques that measure various aspects of the Sun's activity very accurately now appear regularly, but the program begun by Wolf nearly two centuries ago is the longest continuous record of astronomical activity and provides a standard with which nearly all other indices are compared.

The following projects are well underway and will almost certainly bear fruit in the near future. We'll also discuss some diverse uses of solar energy gaining popularity in the U.S. and abroad, and have a little fun speculating about some fanciful proposals.

Spacecraft Exploration

Nowhere is the striking rate of current discovery more evident than in the rapidly expanding use of instruments in space, unimpeded by the effects of Earth's atmosphere. One of the more intriguing new projects is called the Solar and Heliospheric Observatory (SOHO). SOHO will fly at a unique place in space, near the inner Langrangian point, where solar observations can take place continuously without the occasional interruptions caused by the passage of the Earth through the field of observation. The SOHO project will examine the corona and solar wind, and one of its more interesting experiments will be the investigation of long-period vibrations within the Sun's interior using an instrument built and operated by the French.

Close on the heels of the initial SOHO flight, a second spacecraft experiment, the Transitional Region and Coronal Explorer (TRACE) science investigation, will quantitatively explore the connections between fine-scale magnetic fields and their associated plasma structures on the Sun. TRACE will be launched into a Sun-synchronous orbit, which will allow continuous observations for a large portion of the baseline mission. The instrument will collect images of solar plasmas with temperatures from 10,000 to 10,000,000 K degrees, with a spatial resolution of 1 arc second and excellent temporal resolution and continuity.

By flying together in 1997 and 1998, TRACE and SOHO can each gather data sets that are tremendously more valuable than if either were obtained alone. Jointly they will provide the opportunity for simultaneous digital measurements of all the temperature regimes of the Sun's atmosphere using both high resolution imaging and spectroscopy, as well as magnetograms of the photosphere.

During the next few years the Koronas spacecraft will monitor very low frequency radio waves in an attempt to learn even more about solar flares. NASA will continue its studies of the Earth's magnetic field with its Polar spacecraft, complementing the results obtained by Wind, and perhaps finally filling the gaps in our understanding of the terrestrial magnetic field. In addition, and perhaps of equal importance, a number of small, relatively inexpensive Earth explorer satellites will make numerous observations of a number of different aspects of the near-Earth environment and the role the Sun plays in these phenomena.

Just a little farther down the road, around the years 2000 and 2001, when solar activity is expected to be at a high level, the Ulysses spacecraft may be granted a return trip over the Sun's polar regions where it will undoubtedly add to its résumé of exciting discoveries. And NASA's visionary Solar Probe—now a part of the Fire and Ice project, which includes a flyby of the planet Pluto—will measure the Sun's active phenomena from a distance of only a few solar radii.

Other prospective programs include Solar-B and the SPINS/SYSTEMA ecliptic perspective mission. The Mechanisms of Solar Variability initiative has been incorporated into a new program, Solar Connections, and encompasses planning for Solar-B, which will measure the total solar irradiance at high resolution.

However, not all new observations will be provided by future missions or those current flights whose names have become household words for many of us. No discussion of the search for new information would be complete without mention of the extraordinarily productive Pioneer and Voyager spacecraft. These aging space vehicles, which have supplied us with so much information about the giant outer planets and the heliosphere, are now far beyond the orbits of Neptune and Pluto, but they continue to provide exciting revelations about the farthest reaches of the solar system. Eventually these unique craft will pass beyond the heliopause and into interstellar space. It's possible that they will continue to supply us with valuable information about the stellar environment until their faint radio transmissions eventually fade into oblivion.

A Balloon-Borne Experiment

As awe-inspiring and scientifically productive as many spacecraft experiments are, a far less expensive project currently slated to begin in December 1995—the Flare Genesis experiment—ranks with the best of them. Flare Genesis will utilize a stratospheric balloon filled with over 792,000 cubic meters of helium to carry its instruments far above the Earth. The experiment will be launched from the McMurdo Station at the edge of Antarctica. Once adrift, Flare Genesis will ride the counterclockwise winds circling the South Pole at a height of about 40 kilometers for up to 30 days.

Because Earth's magnetic fields open into outer space near the poles, thereby giving cosmic rays and solar particles freer access to the atmosphere, Antarctica has been known as a window on space since the International Geophysical Year (July 1, 1957, through December 31, 1958). The long period of continuous sunlight during the far-austral summer makes the site ideal for suborbital and ground-based scientific experiments. The Flare Genesis project is developed and directed by the Applied Physics Laboratory (APL) at Johns Hopkins University.

The principal aim of Flare Genesis is to determine how the fibrous magnetic fields at the solar surface emerge, coalesce, unravel, and erupt in solar flares. The prototype for the instrument that will obtain these measurements, called the solar vector magnetograph (SVMG), was also designed and built at Johns Hopkins University and is in daily operation at the Sacramento Peak Observatory.

Flare Genesis will use a large, lightweight space-qualified 80-centimeter telescope loaned to APL by the Air Force Phillips Research Laboratory. The telescope was originally designed to visually acquire ballistic missile targets in space, a part of the canceled Star Wars program. From its perch high above the image-blurring layers of Earth's atmosphere, it will provide much better sensitivity for observing the Sun's magnetic fields than the SVMG and other ground-based instruments. The resolution of the primary instrument will allow solar features as small as 0.2 arc second in diameter to be observed, rivaling the best satellite telescopes.

Scientists hope to gain a better understanding of the Earth and its surroundings through such endeavors. The interdisciplinary aspects of these efforts and programs like the SunRISE project, which mate basic science with strategic need, fit well with the current trend of space operations geared toward both astronomical discovery and problem-solving in the terrestrial environment. We have learned our lessons well; interplanetary space is not the only arena to be substantially affected by the Sun's energy.

A Ground-Based Project

Without doubt, the Global Oscillation Network Group (GONG) program—an experiment that seeks to uncover the secrets of the solar interior through a precise investigation of the myriad modes of solar vibration—is the most promising ground-based experiment of the next decade. Since planning and development for this investigation have been underway for a number of years, we outlined the objectives and structure of the GONG program in Chapter 3.

Solar Energy in the Home and Office

Even though there is still an enormous amount to learn about the Sun and its terrestrial effects, some of us are now actively engaged in putting our knowledge to work on Earth. For example, mirroring the attempts of the Anasazi of Pueblo Bonita and the Incas of Machu Picchu, today's progressive builders are erecting structures that make use of passive solar energy, designing them to use as many of Nature's positive attributes as possible.

The characteristics of a passive solar building typically include the use of lots of glass on the northern exposure, less to the east and west where the Sun rises and sets, and a little to the south. A roof overhang projecting toward the south allows light to enter in the winter when the Sun is low in the sky, but limits the amount of entering sunlight in the summer. Alternatively, such structures can be built wholly or partially underground, where they can maintain an almost constant temperature year-round.

Another kind of feature often incorporated into these designs is called an active solar energy system—a highly specialized mechanism that collects the Sun's energy with large panels and uses it to supply the energy requirements for everyday living. The search for an inexpensive but environmentally safe alternative to fossil fuels got a boost in 1973 because of the oil embargo imposed on all industrialized nations by the Organization of Petroleum Exporting Countries. Concerns over pollution caused by the burning of fossil fuels also contributed to this surge of interest, along with the knowledge that these resources are constantly diminishing and will someday be gone entirely.

In Florida, solar water heating and passive cooling have been used since the early part of the 20th century. In fact, by 1930 one out of every two new homes in Florida used solar water heaters. However, as electricity became more available and affordable, solar use waned. Now, however, new agencies such as the Florida Solar Energy Center (FSEC) are hard at work reeducating the public on the benefits and uses of solar power.

The FSEC distributes literature not only to the public but to contractors, engineers, and architects, enabling more homes and offices to be built with solar efficiency in mind. Their diverse package of information includes such items as outlining the methods used to calculate the overhang angle of a southern window based on the site's latitude, and plans for a backyard solar water distiller. Currently, millions of kilowatt hours of electricity are saved in Florida each year through the use of such innovative systems.

Until recently, electric power generated by the most efficient solar panels cost over twice that produced through traditional means. Now, however, at least one manufacturer has developed a special solar panel that can supply all the daytime electric power needed for a home or building for only about half the present costs. The secret of these new panels lies in a special film that can convert sunlight to electricity with an efficiency of over 10 percent, better than the current U.S. government standard for photovoltaic modules designed for widespread application.

In the past, structural heating and cooling together with some methods of generating electric power have provided the lion's share of solar energy uses, but new techniques and materials such as those represented by these high-efficiency solar panels will soon enter the marketplace. To promote such efforts, a number of state governments now offer financial incentives to companies and individuals who develop and employ solar energy technology in their environments.

As you probably suspect, harnessing the Sun's energy is not a new idea. In 1882, a Frenchman named Augustin Mouchot constructed a solar steam engine that powered a printing press. Likewise, John Ericsson, the Swedish-American inventor who designed the first ship with a revolving gun turret, built solar-powered hot air engines. Physicist Robert Goddard, considered by many to be the father of modern American rocketry, long held an interest in solar power. In the 1920s Goddard wrote at least one paper on the use of solar energy with high-altitude rockets and once applied for a patent for a "vaporizer"—a small boiler into which solar energy was directed to convert liquid to water vapor.

When comparing the relative consumer costs of producing energy through conventional and solar means, however, it is not simply a matter of reducing the latter to a 1:1 ratio with the former. Some type of standby power generating system must accompany all such intermittent sources, and this can be expensive where large-scale reliance on non-standard systems is a factor. Such considerations have restricted the use of solar power in the past.

The solar arrays pictured provided heat input for an energy system at the University of Kansas used to heat and cool an apartment building for married students, to furnish hot water for a laundry serving 228 student's families and to supply power to the apartment's electrical system. It was developed by Honeywell, Inc., under NASA contract. The Kansas installation is one of more than 1000 residential, commercial and federal government facilities in a Department of Energy program aimed at national experience, increasing consumer confidence and encouraging more rapid commercialization of solar heating/cooling systems. *Photograph courtesy of NASA.*

Now, however, even in the northern U.S., a growing number of home owners are turning to solar power as a safe, clean, efficient fuel. Popular magazines (see appendix) are beginning to appear with articles on uses of solar energy in the home, including features such as "Designing a Solar System for Homes in Deep Shade," "Using a Suntracker," and "Installing Solar Collectors in Your Home and Business."

Some might not think of the wind as solar power, but the Sun is the source of atmospheric circulation that causes air to move and the wind to blow. And once again an idea from the past is receiving new attention. The Babylonians used windmills to pump water for irrigation in the 17th century B.C., and in 1894 an Arctic explorer named Fridtjof Nansen used a wind generator to charge batteries for electric light. Before the Rural Electrification Administration brought utilities to the remote areas of the American Midwest, windmills were commonly employed to pump water and produce electricity.

The traditional concept of windmill energy uses wind to turn a propeller-like vane. The rapidly revolving vane in turn rotates a shaft that spins the rotor of a power generator. The generator feeds electrical current into either a transmission line or a storage unit. The end result is inexpensive, pollution-free electricity for the windmill owner, with the further advantage that excess amounts of electricity may be sold to local power companies.

Today, such systems operate in the same basic way as those of the past, but modern materials like fiberglass and the light, strong metals developed during the space age are coupled with computer-controlled mechanical systems allowing wind turbines to generate electricity far more efficiently than in the past. Perhaps someday, enormous windmill plantations will cultivate low-cost power on a grand scale.

NASA and the Department of Energy once investigated a potential new source of continuously available energy called the Satellite Power System (SPS). This involved satellites equipped with large solar cell arrays which would convert light energy to electricity, which would, in turn, be converted into microwaves, beamed to Earth to be converted back into electricity and fed directly into the utility network. *Photograph courtesy of NASA.*

Yet another simple and efficient way to utilize solar energy has been in use since the 18th century. Can you guess what it is? It's not surprising if you can't, since until recently this simple device has received only limited attention. Early versions were not always practical and received little use, but now all that has changed. We're thinking about the invention of a Swiss scientist named Horace de Saussure, the solar oven. This clever apparatus effectively employs infrared (heat) energy from the Sun to cook everyday foods. Englishman John Herschel, the equally well-known son of Sir William Herschel and also a talented astronomer, carried one of these neat little stoves with him on his expedition to Africa in 1834.

Now in some third-world countries (particularly those in the tropics), an extraordinary effort is underway to familiarize rural inhabitants with the advantages of solar cookers. Instead of undertaking long daily searches to find wood for cooking as they do today, it may soon be possible to let the natural heat from the Sun provide fuel for family living. It is hoped that the regular use of these devices will slow the destruction of thousands of acres of precious rainforest.

According to the United Nations Food and Agricultural Organization, over 1500 million people are currently affected by fuel-wood shortages. Not only does the solar oven utilize a free fuel source—radiation from the Sun—it also goes

This far-out NASA-JPL Solar Sail spacecraft design was also called heliogyro because of its 12 elongated sails resembling helicopter blades. Each sail blade of the spinning heliogyro (propelled by the Sun's radiation energy) might be over 7 kilometers long to provide maximum power for multiyear flights.
Photograph courtesy of NASA.

about its task without causing pollution. Solar cookers can be used year-round in most of the tropics and during a large part of the year in other sunny areas. (The project section at the end of this chapter contains directions for building a simple, effective solar oven of your own.)

Flights of Fancy

As we move into the next century and venture farther into space it is becoming more and more evident that we must thoroughly understand solar dynamics and use as much as possible of the Sun's virtually limitless energy. As a result, a group of imaginative men and women calling themselves "futurists" (since they study and attempt to predict the course of future events) have proposed a series of innovative schemes that use sunlight for purposes that sometimes border on the exotic.

One concept uses the Sun's radiation to propel specially prepared vehicles through space. If the futurists are correct, such vessels may someday carry people and equipment on everyday trips into the far reaches of the solar system, perhaps to mine ore on a distant planet. They could serve as shuttles between newly developing worlds.

The idea of "solar sailing"—using the minute pressure of sunlight reflected off large sails as a propellant—is not new. The method was originally proposed by the Russian physicist T. S. Tasander in 1924. Since then solar sailing ships have been suggested for such diverse uses as towing small asteroids into Earth's orbit and organized races to the Moon.

Solar sailing is not only the province of the creative futurists. Such systems have been seriously suggested as a power source for asteroid- or comet-bound spacecraft missions. For example, before the return of Halley's Comet in 1986 NASA proposed building a huge solar sail powered vessel named the "Yankee Clipper." NASA designed the Clipper to be a giant solar photon radiation collector, gathering energy to power an attached spacecraft, which would fly in formation with the comet. Although the Clipper was never built, the concept of harnessing the Sun's energy in space continues to be as viable as ever. As far-fetched as the idea appears on the surface, perhaps one day the great ocean-going ships of the past century will be replaced by a regatta of solar sailing ships exploring the sea of space.

Ever since the United States first placed men on its surface in 1969, many of us have dreamed of returning to establish a permanent base on the Moon. The value of a lunar scientific installation could be enormous. Astronomers and other scientists have long desired a permanent observatory, which could be located in a place like the far side of the Moon, away from terrestrial disturbances and unhampered by Earth's atmosphere. A lunar observatory could provide ground-based views of the Sun, solar system, and stars unlike any obtainable from Earth.

The Moon has also been proposed as the site of a futuristic "power tower," a giant solar energy collector located near one of the lunar poles, where sunlight is available almost constantly. This innovative structure could collect solar radiation through a series of solar cells or through a network of mirrors or lenses. A proto-type facility that uses sunlight to convert water to steam, which in turn drives an electrical generator, has been under test near Albuquerque, New Mexico.

A lunar power tower might be designed to beam energy directly to stations on the Earth, route it through special satellites that would transfer the energy to power-hungry cities, or use it at the Moon itself. Without the Earth's winds and comparatively strong gravity, such a device could almost certainly be larger and simpler than a similarly sized tower on Earth.

In the late 1970s, NASA and the U.S. Department of Energy began to study the feasibility of the Satellite Power System (SPS). Projects like the SPS would most likely consist of a satellite with a large solar cell array. The array would collect solar energy, converting it first to electricity and then to microwaves. The satellite's antenna would then beam the microwaves to a ground-based antenna, where they would be reconverted to electricity and distributed as desired.

The problem of dealing with the more dangerous solar radiation remains and must be addressed before we delve deeply into such visionary projects—certainly as we plan a permanent lunar facility or journey to the planets. Space travelers who venture beyond the protection of the Earth's atmosphere must be adequately shielded against potentially fatal doses of X-rays produced in sudden solar eruptions, and as we have seen, delicate instruments are also not immune from their effects.

Although such flights can be planned to take place during times of minimum solar activity, we can't always predict when a major solar storm will occur, and a second type of cosmic radiation—linear energy transfer (LET)—could also present problems. LET particles fragment when they interact with solid matter (such as a spacecraft shield) and create a stream of potentially deadly radiation. Therefore, before we can undertake even a limited exploitation of our cosmic neighborhood, a series of difficult problems must be resolved.

In spite of all we've discovered about the Sun and other astronomical bodies, we are driven to learn more by our inquisitive nature. Along the way, many of us have found that while our knowledge of these objects is considerable, it is far more limited than popularly believed. The journey that uncovers answers to the questions raised by the study of these phenomena promises to be one of excitement, adventure, and challenge. And—on this spaceship at least—there is room for all who would like to join the crew.

An Inexpensive Solar Cooker That Works!

Solar Cookers International (see appendix), a nonprofit, tax-deductible educational organization, is actively working to spread solar cooking skills to all who can benefit from them, particularly those in the fuel-scarce, Sun-rich areas of developing nations. Think of it: a meal cooked without using wood, gas, or any other combustible fuel; a meal cooked using the cleanest, most available (and inexpensive) source of all—the Sun.

Solar cooking is one alternative to traditional fuels that is gaining more and more advocates, both in the U.S. and abroad. The governments of China and India have promoted solar cooking for over a decade, and there are now a reported 100,000 cookers in use in China. In India, one manufacturer, Surya Jyoti Devices, has already produced nearly 500,000 solar cookers. Why? One reason is a current prediction that over 2400 million people will be somehow affected by a shortage of cooking fuels by the year 2000. Such estimates have resulted in a worldwide effort to tackle the problem

simply and inexpensively. Why not join in this effort and fun and build your own solar cooker? (All illustrations courtesy of Solar Cookers International.)

Materials:

- Three cardboard boxes that fit snugly into one another. The boxes should be at least as deep as your cooking utensils are tall. (You may also use two boxes, one slightly larger then the other. Fill any narrow space between their walls and bottoms with small wads of newspaper insulation.)
- A single piece of window glass that is the same shape, but slightly smaller than the inner box
- A large flat piece of cardboard for the oven's lid
- Aluminum foil
- Silicone caulking compound, water-based glue, and some newspaper
- Wood dowel (see below), some string and black priming paint
- A dark metal tray that can fit within the inner box
- Dark-colored cooking utensils with lids

Procedure:

Fit the boxes inside one another. It is very important that the fit be a snug one; if not, fill any space with small wads of crumpled newspaper. If you use the two-box method, be certain to place newspaper insulation between the bottoms of the boxes, as well as around each side. Glue aluminum foil tightly inside the inner box, folding the foil over its top edge. Paint the exterior of the outer box with black paint.

From a piece of cardboard slightly larger than the inner box, cut an interior section

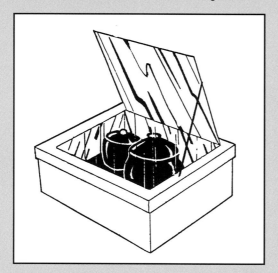

that is a little smaller than the glass. This will eventually act as the frame of the oven's lid—Figure 1. Save the piece of cardboard that you remove to use as a reflector base. Center the lid on top of the cooker so the opening matches the inner box opening; then fold down the edges over the box so the lid fits snugly. Cut, fold and glue the corner flaps. See Figure 2.

Spread caulking compound along the edge of the lid section within the dotted line (Figure 3); then press the window in place firmly to make a good seal. Press flat with a weight until dry.

Glue foil to the piece of cardboard saved for use as the reflector base. Attach one end of a notched wood dowel with string to the corner of the reflector and the other end to the side of the lid—Figure 4.

Place the tray in the inner box and heat the empty solar oven in the Sun for several hours to dry out any moisture (Figure 5).

Cook! Caution: the glass gets very hot!

Basics of Solar Cooking:

Place the cooker outdoors in a place that's sunny for several hours. Put the desired food in a dark utensil with a tight-fitting lid. Aim the reflector toward the Sun and adjust, using the prop, so a maximum amount of sunlight shines into the box. Put the food in the cooker, and cook away! No need to stir.

Meatless Lasagna
(Recipe courtesy Solar Cookers International)
• 1 quart spaghetti sauce
• 1 pound each Ricotta cheese and shredded Mozzarella cheese
• Parmesan cheese
• ½ pound Lasagna noodles

Pour ⅓ of the sauce into the bottom of the roaster pan. Coat the uncooked noodles

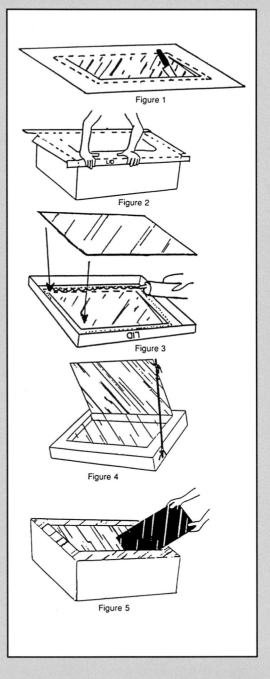

Figure 1

Figure 2

Figure 3

Figure 4

Figure 5

with ricotta cheese and make a bottom layer in the pan. Add half the mozzarella. Repeat to make a second layer, and top with remaining spaghetti sauce and parmesan cheese. Cover and bake 3 hours.

10
Observing the Sun

For most of us, a quick upward glance reveals an apparently unchanging Sun. Day in and day out we watch its journey from east to west, but unlike the ancient Anasazi and Babylonians, we have instruments that allow us to measure its activities and understand its true nature. Moreover, the Sun affords amateur astronomers one of the few remaining opportunities to gather data that is useful to professional scientists.

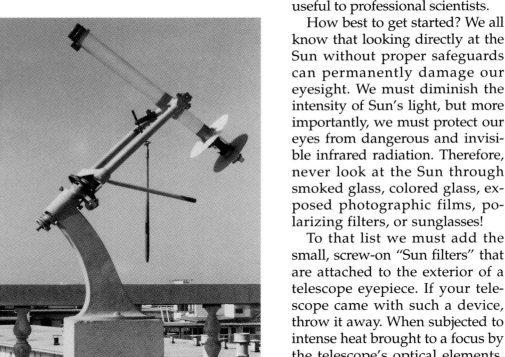

The famous telescope first used by Rudolf Wolf in the mid-19th century. For over 100 years after Wolf's retirement, the instrument was utilized at the Swiss Federal Observatory in Zurich, Switzerland, in the daily observation of the Zurich Relative Sunspot Number. The telescope continues in daily use at the Observatory. *Photograph courtesy of H. U. Keller.*

How best to get started? We all know that looking directly at the Sun without proper safeguards can permanently damage our eyesight. We must diminish the intensity of Sun's light, but more importantly, we must protect our eyes from dangerous and invisible infrared radiation. Therefore, never look at the Sun through smoked glass, colored glass, exposed photographic films, polarizing filters, or sunglasses!

To that list we must add the small, screw-on "Sun filters" that are attached to the exterior of a telescope eyepiece. If your telescope came with such a device, throw it away. When subjected to intense heat brought to a focus by the telescope's optical elements, the filter can suddenly break, exposing your eyes to a full spectrum of dangerous radiation. But in spite of these warnings, remember that there are safe ways to view the Sun both with and without telescopic aid.

Naked-eye observations

Remember, "naked-eye" does not mean "unprotected-eye." To

avoid damage to the eye, use optical filters that reduce the Sun's glare and offer protection from unseen radiation. There are two inexpensive and safe methods for viewing the Sun directly. These are shade #14 welder's glass and the hand-held viewers made of aluminized Mylar commonly called "eclipse glasses." Other than large sunspot groups, you won't be able to see much detail with these methods, but they do offer a low-cost way to see these huge clusters as they traverse the solar disk, and you can get some important data.

You can buy a small square of #14 welder's glass from a supplier of welding materials. Although it is quite appropriate for naked-eye observations, it does not have the necessary quality for use in a telescope's optical system, so its use should be restricted to non-instrumental observations. Roger W. Tuthill Incorporated is a popular source for aluminized Mylar viewers. (Addresses for companies and organizations described in this chapter are listed in the appendix.) You can purchase either item for just a few dollars. Besides observing sunspots, you can use them to monitor the partial phases of a solar eclipse.

In 1984 an international network of naked-eye solar observers was established to compile data about sunspots, and Naked-eye Sunspot Numbers A (A is the symbol for *Auge*, the German word for eye) were introduced for the purpose of statistical analysis.

When considered in the context of an entire sunspot cycle, groups of spots large enough for naked-eye visibility are fairly rare—especially during sunspot minimum, when on more than 90 percent of the days no spots are visible by unaided eye. The amount of these "spotless" days decreases to about 40 percent during maximum, when five to six spots may be seen at one sighting (Figure 10.1).

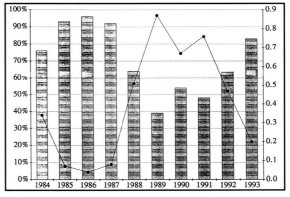

Figure 10.1. Shaded bars: the percentage of days without naked-eye sunspots (left-hand scale); filled circles: yearly means of naked-eye sunspot numbers (right-hand scale). *Diagram courtesy of H. U. Keller.*

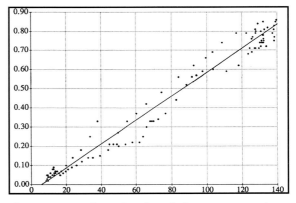

Figure 10.2. Horizontal scale: relative sunspot numbers, R; vertical scale: naked-eye sunspot numbers, A. Filled circles: corresponding values of naked-eye sunspot numbers and relative sunspot numbers (smoothed monthly means). Line: the linear relationship between R and A. *Diagram courtesy of H. U. Keller.*

143

Since the naked-eye network consists of observers with different eye acuity, it is useful to evaluate an average visibility limit for naked-eye sunspots. By measuring the exact sizes of sunspots from telescopic records it is possible to show that spots observed by naked-eye must have a penumbral diameter of at least 40 arc seconds, or about 30,000 kilometers. The approximate linear relationship between naked-eye sunspots (A) and the smoothed relative sunspot number (R) is shown in Figure 10.2.

Using a telescope to observe the Sun

If you want to see the Sun in more detail you'll need to use a telescope, which brings us to the question of which type is best for observing the Sun. You don't have to go out and buy a special telescope to observe the Sun in white light. Virtually any type or size can be used, as long as it has good optical qualities and is solidly constructed. You'll need an electrically driven equatorial mount only if you want to accurately record sunspot positions while projecting the solar image. And bigger is not necessarily better. In fact, the famous Wolf solar telescope, which has been in regular use at the Swiss Federal Observatory in Zurich, Switzerland, for well over 100 years, is a refractor with only 80 millimeters of aperture. The key to high-quality solar observations is not expensive equipment; dedication and patience are the true hallmarks of a quality instrument—and that means you, the observer.

However, in order to make such observations you must protect your eyesight and lower the Sun's brilliance to a comfortable level. We suggest you employ a full-aperture solar filter or use solar projection for this purpose.

Full-aperture solar filters

A full-aperture filter slips over the front of the telescope, reducing the intense heat and light before they can enter. A number of companies offer solar filters for sale, and their advertisements can be found in popular astronomy magazines such as *Astronomy,* but devices with long records of safe and outstanding performance are sold by the Thousand Oaks Optical Company and by the Tuthill organization. Two types of material are commonly used in the manufacture of full-aperture filters: glass and aluminized plastic film called Mylar.

The glass filters manufactured by the Thousand Oaks Company are triple coated with a nickel-chromium alloy. They can be purchased either mounted or unmounted in a wide variety of sizes. Type I and Type II filters are similar, although Type II offers additional durability because it is

A full-aperture solar filter, one of the easiest and safest ways to observe the Sun telescopically. These devices can be purchased mounted or unmounted.

coated with a stainless steel compound. Both produce a pleasing yellow-orange image of the Sun. Thousand Oaks also offers a Type III filter, which is coated to a neutral density of 4 and is intended solely for photographic use.

The widely used Tuthill filters, sold under the trade name Solar Skreen, are produced by combining sheets of aluminized Mylar. They can also be purchased in mounted and unmounted versions and in all popular sizes. Mylar filters are a bit less expensive than similarly-sized glass filters and produce a bluish image of the Sun. If you choose an unmounted Mylar filter, be certain the material is firmly attached to your telescope before beginning observations.

Many observers prefer glass filters because they're more comfortable with a traditionally colored solar image. Moreover, our eyes are more sensitive to detail displayed in the central portion of the visible spectrum. Nevertheless, under some conditions Mylar filters offer a better

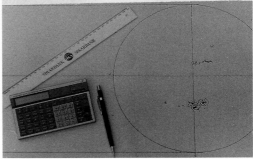

One advantage to the projection method of solar observation is the ease with which the positions of various sunspot groups can be determined using precise drawings. *Photograph courtesy of F. Dubois.*

opportunity to discover detail in features that emit much of their energy toward the blue region of the spectrum, including faculae and certain very intense flares, which we describe later in this chapter. Tuthill says some users add an inexpensive (photographic) Wratten #15 filter when photographing the Sun through a Mylar filter to produce a more natural look. Of course the Wratten filter must never be used without the special solar filter.

Periodically examine any full-aperture filter for damage. If you see pinhole-sized openings while holding the filter up to the light, cover them with small dabs of black paint. If you find a large abraded area, replace the filter. Used as recommended and cared for properly, either type of filter should last for many years.

Some observers, particularly those who view the Sun with large aperture Newtonian-style telescopes, use an aperture mask and sub-diameter filter offset to one side of the telescope opening to decrease its aperture. Some testing is required when experimenting with such a mask, but we suggest stopping to a diameter no larger than 40 to 60 millimeters. Be willing to spend a little time and effort searching for the exact combination of equipment to provide the best results. The Sun will almost always reward you with superb views of its active phenomena.

Solar projection

Projecting the Sun's image onto some type of smooth white surface, the technique first used by Christopher Scheiner in the 17th century, is a simple way to monitor solar activity without the expense of a special filter. Mount a flat, smooth white panel large enough to accept an image about 15 centimeters in diameter in back of the eyepiece.

You can control the diameter of the image either by varying the eyepiece magnification or by changing the distance between the projection screen and eyepiece. The relationship between these components is defined as a

$$\text{distance between surface and eyepiece} = \frac{107d}{m-1} \; ;$$

where m is the eyepiece magnification, and d the desired image diameter expressed in centimeters. The magnification any eyepiece produces varies according to the telescope's focal length. To find it, divide the focal length of the telescope by that of the eyepiece. For instance, a telescope with a focal length of 90 centimeters would require an eyepiece with a focal length of 15 millimeters in order to produce a magnification of 60x.

Simple arithmetic demonstrates that an image diameter of 15 centimeters can be obtained with an eyepiece that produces 60x and an eyepiece-to-projection screen distance of about 27 centimeters. Since the distance between the Sun and Earth changes a little during the year, make some provision so the screen's position relative to the eyepiece can be varied slightly. Once you achieve the correct diameter image you can bring it to maximum sharpness with the telescope's focusing device, just as you would while looking through the eyepiece under normal circumstances.

When projecting the Sun's image, the darker the area into which it is projected, the more detail you'll see. So if you mount a screen in an area exposed to direct sunlight, install a shade near the front of the telescope that throws a shadow on the projection surface. Some observers attach the projection screen directly to the telescope, but you can get better images by mounting it separately. When following this method, select an eyepiece with care. The Sun's heat can soften the cement holding some optical components together, so choose a type that does not use such construction methods (such as a Ramsden).

The Sun's image can also be projected, as shown in this photograph. When this method is used on a regular basis, the projection screen should be rigidly mounted, and the image projected into the darkest location that is available. *Photograph courtesy of Photographer, Ken Spencer.*

146

You can also project the solar image onto a surface enclosed in a projection box that has an open port for observations. If you cover the interior of the box (other than the projection surface) with white felt or a similar coating (some experts recommend black), you can keep most stray light away from the projected image and see more detail. If you attach the box directly to the telescope, additional counterweights may be required. In any event, keep the box as lightweight as possible.

Tracing the projected sunspot images onto a sheet of paper temporarily attached to the screen can give some idea as to their size. For example, if the image diameter is 15 centimeters and a group of spots located near the middle of the disk has a length of 3 millimeters (that is, $\frac{1}{50}$ the image diameter), it indicates, based on an actual solar diameter of 1,392,630 kilometers, that the group is nearly 28,000 km across—twice the diameter of the Earth! (Because of foreshortening, this simple method will not work for groups located away from the disk center; for them, you'll have to use a little spherical trigonometry.)

Another advantage of the projection method, in addition to its absolute safety, is that a number of people can view the Sun at one time. Consequently this method is the one most often used by teachers and parents who guide their students and children as they track large sunspots. You may want to try projecting the Sun's image through binoculars if you don't have a telescope. Simply cover one objective lens and project the Sun's image as if you were using a regular telescope. Of course, in this case you probably won't use the equation and you will have to experiment with image size and focus.

When, where, and how to observe the Sun

Many experienced solar observers believe the best time of day for serious observations is around midmorning, before the Sun has heated the atmosphere but after it is high enough in the sky that the observer can avoid viewing through an excessively thick atmosphere. Failing that, late afternoon usually offers the next best time. The goal is to find the time of day when the layer of atmosphere nearest the ground is steadiest.

Since the Sun heats everything it touches, you will be making observations through unsteady, heated air reflected from houses, walls, pavement, and sidewalks. You can minimize these problems if you choose your observing site as carefully as the time you make observations. If your telescope is portable, erect it well away from large structures and paved areas. A grassy area is a good choice, or better still, a site near a body of water. In fact, experts did just that when they built the solar observatory at Big Bear, California, on an island in the middle of a small lake.

Once your equipment is set up the first order of business is to cover the finder's objective lens. This will prevent an uninitiated bystander—and they are encountered frequently when observing the Sun—from accidental eye damage. Keep in mind that children are particularly vulnerable and it is the telescope owner's responsibility to ensure the safety of interested spectators and others who gather around the instrument.

But with no finder, how do you place the Sun in the field of view? Simply point the telescope toward the Sun and arrange the tube so its shadow is as small as possible. A few careful adjustments made while glancing through the eyepiece will bring the image into view where it can be brought to a fine focus using a conveniently located group of spots or, failing that, the Sun's limb. You may find yourself readjusting the focus slightly as heat warms the telescope's optics and as you move from features located near the central zone to those closer to the limb, since the Sun is so large.

Begin your observations with a low magnification that allows you to see the entire solar disk at once, and then move up to 60 or 65x. After you gain some experience with your telescope and local seeing conditions you will have a good idea of how powerful a magnification is possible for you. On those rare days when the atmosphere is extraordinarily steady you may be able to use a very powerful amplification—perhaps in the range of 200x. More often, however, because of atmospheric anomalies such magnifications will actually show less detail than the typical 60 to 65x.

What can you see?

Although naked-eye techniques limit an observer to the observation and movements of large sunspot groups, a wealth of small detail opens to the telescopic observer. As you probably suspect, the most noticeable features are almost always those notorious sunspots. These regions of the Sun are dominated by one or more dark-looking areas known as "umbrae."

Sometimes sunspot groups consist of a solitary spot (umbra), and sometimes they become very complex and contain more than 100 individual spots. One or more less-dark regions—penumbrae—frequently surround the umbrae. When the observing conditions are good, penumbrae often display an amazing amount of detail, including an intricate network of faint line-like filaments. Such features radiate outward in a regular pattern when they appear with large circular spots, but are nonradial and irregular when associated with complex spot groups.

Hot bright patches of hydrogen gas—the photospheric faculae—can often be seen near groups of sunspots. Faculae indicate high magnetic activity and therefore often foretell the appearance of a new group of spots. An observational phenomenon called "limb-darkening" provides the contrast that allows faculae to appear brighter when near the limb. Limb-darkening is precipitated by our oblique view through the cooler portion of upper photosphere as the limb is neared, and is intensified by the heating effects inherent in magnetic phenomena.

Many observers will quickly note that rather than appear as a smooth globe, the entire solar surface has a rough appearance—the so-called "rice grain" effect—caused by groups of convective cells bursting through the outer layers of the Sun. Occasionally, when the atmospheric conditions are excellent and a moderate-size telescope is available, you may be able to glimpse clusters of these solar granules near the center of the disk (see photo, Chapter Two).

Furthermore, if you combine a little knowledge with a great deal of luck (about the same amount it would take to win the lottery), you might, like Carrington, just be fortunate enough to see a solar white-light flare (WLF). Flares generally occur in or around sunspot groups, but they can be seen only rarely without special equipment. (These huge bursts of energy are regularly seen when observed within the hydrogen-alpha spectral line, as described later.) However, several times during each solar cycle an extraordinarily bright flare occurs, which can be seen in white light through a standard solar filter like the ones we've discussed.

Because flares result from sudden changes in a magnetic field, it's much more likely you'll see a WLF near large and complex spot groups—known regions of unstable magnetic activity. When solar activity is high be especially alert for large asymmetric groups that are completely surrounded by penumbra and contain numerous small spots. These groups are the most likely sources of WLFs which, seen in white light, appear as exceptionally bright patches that last a few minutes at best. As we've said previously, the blue-tinged image generated by a Mylar filter may increase your chance of seeing such a flare.

Once in a while a portion of large umbrae will appear to be divided by a thin strip of bright solar material—a light-bridge—which lasts for several days and often signals the onset of the group's demise. Observations near the limb often reveal a connection between a light-bridge and photospheric faculae. Novice observers often confuse such features with a white-light solar flare, but if you remember that a flare will only be visible for a few minutes, you won't be confused.

Can all these features be seen while using the projection method? Although sunspot groups and phenomena such as limb darkening are easily detected when using projection, some fine details may be missing. If you decide to use the projection method, place the projection screen in as dark an area as possible. Under good conditions you will be able to see spots, faculae, and a glimpse or two of the Sun's granular structure. And somewhat surprisingly, many white-light flares have been observed while using this procedure.

Counting those enigmatic sunspots

Sunspot counting is one of the more interesting ways amateur astronomers can become familiar with the Sun while also collecting data that can be useful to the scientific community. Once you gain some expertise you may find the accumulation of such data addictive. Remember, however, that for such data to be scientifically useful it must be gathered according to strict criteria and compiled by one of the few organizations that regularly supply such information to professionals (see appendix).

Sunspot observers operate a little differently from other astronomers. The organizations that compile spot numbers do so daily, so most of their contributors try to observe the Sun even when weather is marginal. And they are observers in the true sense—less concerned with the construction of their equipment than with its use. Still, good estimates of sunspot activity are hard to get and newcomers are occasionally confused by the arcane way this procedure has been explained through the years.

Use two eyepiece magnifications when counting sunspots. Initially, select a low magnification that allows you to view the entire disk at one time. With this

149

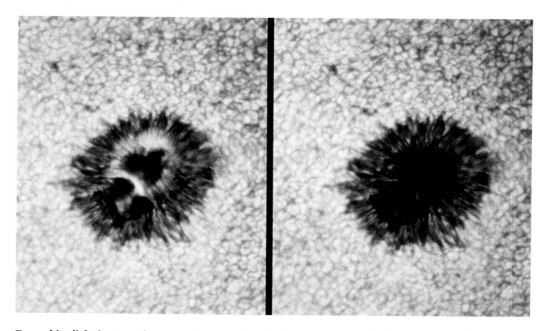

Two white-light images of a sunspot group, using different exposures, obtained by Dr. William Livingston during excellent seeing conditions at the McMath-Pierce Telescope—Kitt Peak. One view is a conventional picture of a unipolar group near the center of the solar disk on a full-disk magnetogram with an exposure of 1/500 second. Note the light bridge suspended over the umbra. The other view is the same but overprinted with umbral information from an exposure of 1/150 second, showing fibrous intrusions which delineate still darker areas. When such images are combined, the umbra is resolved into an filamentary structure connected to the penumbra. *Photographs courtesy of the NOAO/ National Solar Observatories.*

eyepiece, ferret out all (or nearly all) of the spot groups and locate them on a small disk drawing. Such sketches, perhaps 1 or 2 inches in diameter, should be very simple. They provide a guide to the location of the smaller groups on days after their first appearance and furnish a record of group evolution.

The second eyepiece should provide the recommended magnification of 65x. This degree of amplification has been found to be ideal for sunspot counting and also for finding those faint and therefore elusive spot groups which separate the expert from a run-of-the-mill observer.

After all groups of spots are located, count the individual spots within each group and record the total directly on the drawing next to the appropriate cluster. Add any newly uncovered groups to the sketch. After completing observations for the day, combine these data into the daily sunspot estimate, R, with

R = 10g + s;

where g is the number of groups, and s the total number of spots. (This relationship was originally established by Rudolf Wolf in the mid-19th century. Wolf referred to the series as "universal" rather than "relative" sunspot numbers.)

For example, if you can see two small groups consisting of 1 and 2 spots respectively, and a larger group of 16 spots, the estimate for that day is 49 (3 groups times 10, plus 19 separate spots). Enter that information along with the date and time of the observation.

This brings us to a major problem for many novice sunspot counters—finding the smallest, and therefore most elusive, spot groups. Unfortunately these clusters often make up a large portion of those on the disk, so their discovery is very important. This is

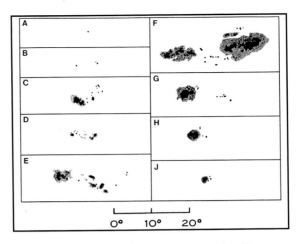

Figure 10.3. The Zurich sunspot group classifications, types A-H and J. Note the evolutionary nature of the growth (A-F) and decay (G-H and J) of sunspot groups.

especially true near the minimum of a solar cycle, when such groups may be the only spots visible. A good way to minimize this problem is to systematically scan the entire disk at least three times, noting each group as you progress. While engaged in this routine you may encounter a common but always surprising characteristic of solar observing. The observer carefully searches the Sun's disk, recording each new area of sunspot activity. Then on a second or third examination, an additional group, absolutely undetected during previous observations, suddenly appears. Early solar observers believed they had witnessed the birth of a new group of spots when this occurred. However, the phenomenon is more likely a physiological effect, possibly related to some idiosyncrasy of the human eye or eye-brain mechanism.

In any event, after an initial search of the disk, closely inspect the Sun's limb. You might spot a new group as it begins its rotation onto the visible hemisphere or glimpse the last vestiges of an old cluster as the group completes its transit of the western limb. Observations of these groups count too!

Heliographic latitudes outside the normal sunspot zone (a circumsolar band extending approximately 35 degrees north and south of the Sun's equator) can also prove to be fruitful hunting grounds. Every so often during most cycles a group will appear at an abnormally high latitude. Such clusters are generally simple and short-lived, but they offer the challenge of discovery, which in turn helps ensure an accurate record.

Just what constitutes a group? Sunspot growth and decline is evolutionary, and the clusters can be divided into types with certain general characteristics. Not all groups pass through all classifications, but all begin as tiny members of class A, when newly emerging magnetic flux penetrates the photosphere. These groups may be short-lived—lasting for less than a day—or they may grow into huge

151

collections of individual spots that endure for several solar rotations. Most groups quickly evolve into bipolar configurations made up of two main spots oriented in a rough east-west direction. Examples of each group type (A through H and J) are shown in Figure 10.3. Remember that groups in each category can take a variety of forms and still retain their basic characteristics, and that the continuously changing face of the Sun will present difficult group conglomerations from time to time.

Now, if you've been bitten by the solar bug and want to see even more of the Sun's spectacular features—the giant loops of gas called prominences and the finest surface detail—you'll need to add another piece of equipment to your arsenal: a neat little device known as a hydrogen-alpha filter.

The majesty of Hydrogen-alpha

Observing the Sun within a specific wavelength of visible light was once the exclusive province of the professional astronomer. But devices that enable such observations have been greatly improved, and their price has dropped significantly. Consequently, an increasing number of amateur astronomers are enjoying the sensational views possible only when viewing the Sun this way. Since these are highly specialized solar observations, we asked an expert, William Winkler, to tell us a little about his equipment and techniques. Here's what Bill had to say:

A view of the Sun's disk in which all but the light emitted by singly ionized hydrogen has been blocked is among the most spectacular sights in all astronomy. You can see complicated and esthetically pleasing detail both on the disk and just beyond its limb at even the quietest part of the sunspot cycle, and significant changes occur during a single observing session. Still and video photography of this detail (monochromatic photographs are called filtergrams), seen in shades of gray and a wide variety of deep-red brightnesses, is also rewarding. Like more conventional observations of the Sun, narrow-band solar observation is done without regard to light pollution or haze and during relatively warm temperatures without losing sleep. All this is the majesty of hydrogen-alpha (Hα).

If you become a committed solar observer and want to do more than observe in white light, your next step is to obtain equipment that will allow observations in an extremely narrow part of the visible spectrum. By far the most prominent optical spectral line is the H I, or "alpha" line of singly ionized hydrogen, centered near 6563 angstroms (Å). It is easiest to obtain narrow-band instruments for this line—deep in the red—and a great deal of visible astrophysics is revealed in the Sun's Hα emissions.

In white light, the photosphere is revealed with its sunspot umbrae and penumbrae, faculae, and faint granulation. The Sun appears to have a sharp edge and prominent limb-darkening. For a few years centered on sunspot cycle maximum the white-light Sun is visually spectacular, but for those years around cycle minimum there is far less activity to observe, and during a single observing period very little change can be detected.

But in Hα—an examination of the solar disk in a portion of a spectral line less than 1Å wide—the thicker and hotter chromosphere is exposed with its large bright areas (plage), occasional intensely bright areas (flares), dark filaments of various lengths and widths (prominences seen projected against the disk), and complex network of fibrils and superpenumbral filaments—elements that are much larger and longer-lived than cells of photospheric granulation. Near sunspots and plage these features spiral in towards centers of activity much as iron filings do near a magnet. In fact, it is believed that fibrils connect areas of opposite magnetic polarity, aligning themselves along local magnetic fields. The solar limb is not sharp in Hα but appears as a well-defined region of short-lived, tiny flamelike spicules.

Usually several much larger and longer-lasting structures can be seen projecting far above this region. In the main these are prominences seen in profile, great columns of cooler gases held in place by looping magnetic fields. During an eclipse prominences are usually seen in whitelight as features with a brilliant pink color. In Hα, however, they appear dull or bright red with dark "feet" seen projected against the solar disk. Sunspot umbrae are apparent in Hα, but most penumbrae lose their white-light appearance. Except for solar flares, a rich variety of chromospheric activity is present even near sunspot minimum and a great deal of change can be seen within each observing period.

A fully assembled hydrogen-alpha filter unit attached to a portable 10-centimeter aperture refracting telescope decreases its effective aperture to a little over 6 centimeters. The cable runs to a 12-volt Port-a-Pac rechargeable battery which powers the filter heater. Photograph courtesy of W. Winkler.

Observing the Sun in Hα is certainly more expensive and time-consuming in setup than conventional solar observing, but it offers a lifetime of fascination. Hα observation adds a vertical dimension to, and complements, white-light viewing, and to most of us is well worth the effort and expense.

Except for professional observatories and a few wealthy amateurs who use spectrohelioscopes, all Hα solar disk observations are obtained with interference filters. Such a filter uses a series of vaporized metal layers applied with extreme precision to optical glass. It is located at the focus of an optical system with a focal ratio of at least 1:30.

A red glass filter placed over the aperture blocks certain other wavelengths that the Hα filter can transmit and prevents the telescope and filter from overheating. The wavelength passed by the Hα filter can be varied somewhat by controlling its temperature and tilt from perpendicular to the optical axis of the telescope. Birefringent filters (such as the Lyot filter) can be made with a series of optical quartz plates of increasing thickness separated by polarizers, but these are generally impractical for amateur and portable use.

In the United States only the DayStar Filter Corporation makes affordable Hα filters for amateur observations (the DayStar company also manufactures instruments for professional use). When ordering such a device, purchasers supply their telescopes' specifications, give the temperature range over which their filter will be used, and choose a band width. To view detail on the disk the latter should be between 0.8 and 0.5Å. The narrower band widths are more expensive but provide higher contrast.

The DayStar company then manufactures a filter with appropriate characteristics and associated optics (Barlow extender-lens, extension tubes, tilt and temperature controls, objective mask, and red filter). The filter, when inserted into the telescope draw-tube, produces an f/30 Hα system for safe direct viewing. Why f/30? Faster ratios broaden an Hα filter's bandwidth or shift the transmission peak, resulting in a loss of contrast and detail. A star diagonal and long-focus eyepiece or camera body can be plugged directly into the filter unit.

Photo 10.13 shows the parts of a typical 0.7Å DayStar Hα filter system for use with a f/10 refracting telescope of 100-millimeter aperture. It has a tilt knob and thermostat-controlled heater. Photo 10.14 shows the unit attached to the telescope in portable use. I recommend an f/10 or higher-ratio refractor with at least an 80-millimeter diameter lens, or a Cassegrain/Schmidt-Cassegrain reflector of at least 200-millimeter aperture, since with the latter telescopes the aperture stop and red filter must be installed off-axis. Telescopes of the Newtonian type are not suitable. Seek advice from DayStar or one of their dealers, but I believe you will find a 0.7Å or narrower band-width filter with built-in heater, thermostat, and tilt control to your liking. (All optical interference filters are very sensitive to temperature changes and should be regulated by a heating device.)

One part of the fascination of solar Hα observation is the rapid change that takes place in various features; another is the Doppler effect. As you scan the disk and limb prominences, motions within some features are often significant enough that they are centered in different portions of the blue or red "wings" of the Hα line. Because parts of the highly magnified disk are most prominent in different portions of the line, some features may change their appearance as the solar image moves through the field of view in right ascension or declination, or as you center a different portion of the spectral line by tilting the filter.

A third part of this absorbing process is three dimensional. By tuning back and forth from well within the Hα line to somewhere outside it you can compare the location of high-altitude chromospheric features with those far below at the photospheric level. And the day may come when you will happen upon an especially large and intensely bright solar flare only to learn later that it was associated in some way with effects on Earth.

During our hot Texas summers I find that about ten minutes after I turn on the filter heater (with the unit already installed on the telescope and aimed at the Sun) the view changes from a red disk with sunspots and sharp limb to a disk rich in detail, replete with prominences and a well-defined jagged edge of spicules. At some point the heater (powered by 12-volt battery or AC) can be switched off for a few minutes and the passband maintained by filter tilt, but detail ultimately disappears unless the heater is reactivated. You will probably find that a Plössl-type eyepiece with a focal length of around 32 millimeters is a good starting point for most Hα observations.

If you have a lifetime interest in solar observing, the expense of a Hα filter will seem small when compared with the captivating views you receive. Is such a device for you? Ask yourself if your lifestyle will permit you to observe the Sun other than on weekends. Weekend-only viewing may not justify the cost of a unit; perhaps you should wait until later in life. Could you use a portable unit at work during lunch, storing it in your car? Do you have a suitable telescope that can be modified to produce an f/30 beam, or will that be an additional expense?

For many years I wanted to observe the Sun regularly in Hα. I had planned to postpone this dream until retirement but as filter prices slowly decreased and my teaching hours permitted observations on weekdays I realized I was missing a great deal by observing the Sun only in white light. The variances of health and finances being as they are, I decided to make the move to the majesty of hydrogen-alpha now. It's been great.

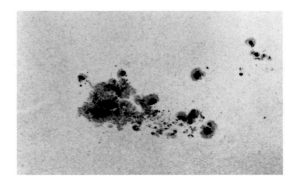

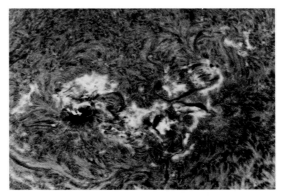

Two striking views of a large sunspot group. The upper image was taken in white light and the lower photograph was obtained shortly afterward using a narrow-band (0.6Å) hydrogen-alpha filter. *Photographs courtesy of J. Dragesco, la Riviere, France.*

Radio observations

You can observe the Sun both directly and indirectly by monitoring certain radio frequencies. For example, solar flare-induced ionospheric anomalies can be recorded by monitoring very low frequency (18 to 30 kilohertz) radio signals. Changes in the signal's transmission strength occur in real time as a result of the X-ray emission produced in many flares. The events, known as sudden ionospheric disturbances, are recorded with simple receivers that output the fluctuations to small strip-chart recorders or personal computers for later analysis. Such data are used regularly by astronomers and ionospheric researchers. The AAVSO Solar Division coordinates the largest effort of this type in the world today and will be happy to supply the details of this program to interested individuals.

The Sun also emits longer-wave radio signals, which amateurs can monitor with relatively simple antennas and receivers. In simplest format the antenna terminal of a regular shortwave receiver with a frequency range of 1 to 30 megahertz is connected to a loop antenna via an inexpensive radio frequency preamplifier. The output of the receiver is connected to a detector and integrator circuit, which is in turn attached to a recording device. The Society of Amateur

Radio Scientists will supply information to those who would like to observe the Sun in this interesting manner.

Observing solar eclipses

Although you must use the special observing equipment we have described for normal solar observations during most of an eclipse (that is, welder's glass, solar filters, or the projection method), for the few minutes of totality when no bright photosphere is visible you can safely view the Sun without protection. And what a sight it is! The corona, usually totally obscured by sunlight, can be seen in all its glory, and prominences—some of them hundreds of thousands of kilometers long—may spout from the Sun's surface. Some observers use this time to look for the inner planets, Mercury and Venus, or to search for comets (in the 19th century, a comet was actually discovered during a total solar eclipse). However, be certain to keep track of time. You don't want to be caught staring directly at the Sun when the photosphere suddenly reemerges with the brilliant flash of diamond ring.

Even though you can only see such solar phenomena during a total eclipse, annular eclipses are still well worth observing. During an annular eclipse the Moon is far enough away from the Earth that it can't completely cover the Sun, but an observer near the line of central eclipse often witnesses a spectacular band of sunlight surrounding the Moon—the so-called "ring of fire." And if the Moon's disk is only a little smaller than the Sun's, Baily's beads may also appear. Even with the Sun only partially covered, a noticeable drop in temperature and eerie twilight frequently occur. Remember, however, that during a partial or annular eclipse, it is never safe to view the Sun without suitable protection.

Basic solar photography

At some point most solar observers try their hand at solar photography. And those of us fortunate enough to view an eclipse of the Sun almost always want to record the experience. Photographing astronomical objects is a subject onto itself; therefore, we will describe a few basic techniques designed to get you off to a good start and let experience and research take it from there.

Most of us have access to a 35-millimeter camera, an excellent device for photographing the Sun. Remember, however, that like the human eye your camera must be protected from the intense heat of the Sun; you must use a suitable filter at all times. Place a Mylar or glass solar filter, or a series of neutral density filters with a total density rating of 4 or 5 over the lens. The latter must completely cover the camera lens; they are stacked one on top of another to produce a desired density (for example, ND 1.0 and 4.0 filters can be combined to produce a ND rating of 5.0).

Image size is a function of focal length, so choose a lens with the longest possible focal length. The standard 50-millimeter lens will yield a basically useless image only 0.5 millimeter in diameter. But if you use one of the relatively new catadioptric or mirror lenses (focal lengths generally around 500 millimeters), the image will grow to a diameter of about 4.6 millimeters, and if you add a 2x teleconverter that size will double. The key here is that for any particular focal length, the diameter of the Sun's image will be approximately equal to the focal length divided by 109.

Follow a similar procedure if you plan to use your telescope for solar photography. If you project the Sun's image, mount the camera to one side of the telescope, shade the image as much as possible, and photograph it as it is displayed on the projection screen. In this situation, a light meter will be helpful in determining exposure times.

If you wish to photograph the Sun directly through the telescope, use a regular solar filter (or one especially designed for solar photography, such as the Thousand Oaks Type III). In this case, it's simplest to remove the camera lens and replace it with an adapter that allows the camera to be coupled to the eyepiece holder with the eyepiece removed. These accessories are inexpensive, easy to install, and can be purchased from companies such as Edmunds Scientific Company.

When you wish to photograph the entire disk of the Sun within a single frame, the 35-millimeter film frame size dictates a telescope focal length of 260 centimeters or shorter. Longer focal lengths will allow only a portion of the disk to be recorded. Regardless of instrument, select a slow to medium film speed because available light is not a problem when photographing the Sun. Experiment with different film and shutter speeds, as well as exposure times, for the best results.

Table 10.1, originally published in NASA Reference Publication 1318, provides a good guide for combinations of these parameters. During any tests (and while photographing an eclipse) it is a good idea to bracket the listed exposure times, especially for the type of phenomena that are of particular interest. Remember that during the total phase of a total solar eclipse, *and only then,* is all filtering removed. When you wish to photograph the corona, keep focal lengths no longer than 150 to 180 centimeters. Otherwise, during the longer exposures a portion of the Sun's atmosphere may be cut off by the 35-millimeter frame size.

At least one US organization—the Solar Section of the Association of Lunar and Planetary Observers—has compiled an extensive library of solar photographs obtained in both white light and discrete wavelengths (primarily Hα). Such photos, recorded by experienced amateur solar photographers and obtained according to specific guidelines, can be useful to professional solar astronomers. See the appendix for more information.

Last but not least, one association—the Society for Amateur Scientists (SAS)—exists for the express purpose of enabling amateur scientists and astronomers to work directly with professionals in bonafide research projects. The SAS participates in activities in a number of different scientific fields, gathering and analyzing data, and publishing the results in various journals. Serious amateur scientists are urged to contact the SAS office for further details.

Table 10.I. A guide to solar photography.
Reprinted from Nasa Reference Publication 1318.

Solar Photogaphic Exposure Guide

ISO	f/Number								
25	1.4	2	2.8	4	5.6	8	11	16	22
50	2	2.8	4	5.6	8	11	16	22	32
100	2.8	4	5.6	8	11	16	22	32	44
200	4	5.6	8	11	16	22	32	44	64
400	5.6	8	11	16	22	32	44	64	88
800	8	11	16	22	32	44	64	88	128
1600	11	16	22	32	44	64	88	128	176

Subject	Shutter Speed								
Solar Eclipse									
Partial-4.0 ND	—	—	—	1/4000	1/2000	1/1000	1/500	1/250	1/125
Partial-5.0 ND	1/4000	1/2000	1/1000	1/500	1/250	1/125	1/60	1/30	1/15
Baily's Beads[1]	—	—	—	—	1/4000	1/2000	1/1000	1/500	1/250
Chromosphere	—	—	—	1/4000	1/2000	1/1000	1/500	1/250	1/125
Prominences	—	1/4000	1/2000	1/1000	1/500	1/250	1/125	1/60	1/30
Corona-0.1 Rs	1/2000	1/1000	1/500	1/250	1/125	1/60	1/30	1/15	1/8
Corona-0.2 Rs[2]	1/500	1/250	1/125	1/60	1/30	1/15	1/8	1/4	1/2
Corona-0.5 Rs	1/125	1/60	1/30	1/15	1/8	1/4	1/2	1 sec	2 sec
Corona-1.0 Rs	1/30	1/15	1/8	1/4	1/2	1 sec	2 sec	4 sec	8 sec
Corona-2.0 Rs	1/15	1/8	1/4	1/2	1 sec	2 sec	4 sec	8 sec	15 sec
Corona-4.0 Rs	1/8	1/4	1/2	1 sec	2 sec	4 sec	8 sec	15 sec	30 sec
Corona-8.0 Rs	1/2	1 sec	2 sec	4 sec	8 sec	15 sec	30 sec	1 min	2 min

ND—Neutral Density filter
Rs—Solar Radii

Notes:
[1] Baily's Beads are extremely bright and change rapidly.
[2] This exposure also recommended for the "Diamond Ring" effect.
The un-eclipsed Sun should be photographed according to the parameters listed for partial eclipse.
(From NASA Reference Publication 1318, F. Espenak, 1992.)

Appendix

Organizations of Interest

Association of Lunar and
Planetary Observers
Solar Section
Paul Maxson
8839 North 30th Avenue
Phoenix, AZ 85051

American Association of
Variable Star Observers
Solar Division
Peter O. Taylor
4523 Thurston Lane, #5
Madison, WI 53711-4738
Internet:
ptaylor@NGDC.NOAA.GOV

British Astronomical
Association
Head Office
Burlington House
Piccadilly, London W1V
9AG
United Kingdom
071-734-4145

British Sundial Society
Barncroft, Grizebeck
Kirby-in-Furness
Cumbria LA17 7XJ
United Kingdom

Chaco Culture National
Historic Park
National Park Service
505-786-7014

Florida Solar Energy Center
300 State Road 401
Cape Canaveral, FL 32920
407-783-0300
(solar planning information
and software)

Irish Tourist Board
800-223-6470
(to arrange a visit to the
Newgrange Tomb)

Livesay, R. J.
BAA Aurora Section
Flat 1/2
East Parkside
Edinburgh EH16 5XJ
Scotland

Museum of Northern Arizona
Flagstaff, AZ
602-774-5211
(Native American Cultures of
the American Southwest)

Naked-Eye Sunspot
Observations
H. U. Keller
Kolbenhofstrasse 33
CH-8045 Zurich
Switzerland

North American Sundial
Society
Fred Sawyer
8 Sachem Drive
Glastonbury, CT 06033

Royal Astronomical Society
Burlington House
London, W1V 0NL
United Kingdom
071-734-4582

Rudolf Wolf Gesellschaft
H. U. Keller, Secretary
Kolbenhofstrasse 33
CH-8045 Zurich,
Switzerland

(The Rudolf Wolf Gesellschaft
aims at securing the continua-
tion of the Zurich sunspot
observations with Wolf's original telescope at the former
Swiss Federal Observatory in
Zurich. For this purpose and
to preserve and catalog the
archives of the Zurich Observatory, the society endeavors
to procure the financial support necessary to establish an
independent institution.)

Society of Amateur Radio
Astronomers, Inc.
Vince Caracci, Membership
Services
247 North Linden Street
Massapequa, NY 11758
516-798-8459

Society for Amateur
Scientists
Shawn Carlson
4951 Claremont Square,
Ste. 179
San Diego, CA 92117
800-873-8767
Internet: scarlson@sas.org

Solar Cookers International
1724 Eleventh Street
Sacramento, CA 95814
916-444-6616
Fax: 916-444-5379
Internet: SBCI@igc.apc.org

Solar Town Center
Soldiers Grove, WI 54655
608-624-5209

Products and Supplies of Interest

Edmund Scientific
101 East Gloucester Pike
Barrington, NJ 08007
609-547-8880
Fax: 609-573-6295
(prisms, solar projects)

Edwin Hirsch
29 Lakeview Drive
Tomkins Cove, NY 10986
914-786-3738
(DayStar hydrogen-alpha
solar filters and related
equipment)

Orion Telescope Center
800-447-1001
Fax: 408-464-0466
(eyepieces equipped with
cross-hair reticle)

Software Bisque
912 Twelfth Street, Suite A
Golden, CO 80401
800-843-7599
Fax: 303-278-0045
(Astronomy software. For
other commercial software,
see popular astronomy
publications.)

Thousand Oaks Optical
Box 4813
Thousand Oaks, CA 91359
805-996-9111
Fax: 805-491-2393
(glass full-aperture solar
filters)

Roger W. Tuthill, Inc.
Box 1086 Q
11 Tanglewood Lake
Mountainside, NJ 07092
908-232-1786
Fax: 908-232-3804
(full-aperture Mylar solar filters and related equipment)

Publications of Interest

Astronomy magazine
Kalmbach Publishing Co.
21027 Crossroads Circle
Waukesha, WI 53187
800-533-6644

Sky Bear Publishing
10464 Clairemont Mesa
Blvd., #222
San Diego, CA 92124
(amateur astronomy
newsletter)

Communications Quarterly
76 North Broadway
Hicksville, NY 11801
603-664-2515
(solar astronomy column;
amateur radio information)

Home Power
"The Hands-On Journal of
Home-Made Power"
Box 520
Ashland, OR 97520
916-475-0830

Sky and Telescope magazine
Box 9111
Belmont, MA 02178
800-253-0245

Solar Today magazine
2400 Central, Unit G-1
Boulder, CO 80301
303-443-3130

Suggestions for Further Reading

Dragesco, J. 1995, *High-
Resolution Astrophotogra-
phy,* Cambridge University
Press.

Hargreaves, J. K. 1992, *The
Solar-Terrestrial Environ-
ment,* Cambridge University
Press (ISBN 0-521-32748-2).

Phillips, K. J. H. 1992, *Guide
to the Sun,* Cambridge
University Press
(ISBN 0-521-39483-X).

Taylor, P.O. 1991, *Observ-
ing the Sun,* Cambridge
University Press
(ISBN 0-521-40110-0).

Zirin, H. 1988, *Astrophysics
of the Sun,* Cambridge
University Press
(ISBN 0-521-302684).

Contacting the Authors by Electronic Mail

Peter O. Taylor
Internet:
ptaylor@NGDC.NOAA.GOV

Nancy L. Hendrickson
CompuServe: 73557,2602
Internet: nhendr@cts.com

Index